FEAR ITSELF

# Fear Itself

*The Causes and Consequences of Fear in America*

Christopher D. Bader, Joseph O. Baker,
L. Edward Day, and Ann Gordon

NEW YORK UNIVERSITY PRESS
New York

NEW YORK UNIVERSITY PRESS
New York
www.nyupress.org
© 2020 by New York University
All rights reserved

Library of Congress Cataloging-in-Publication Data
Names: Bader, Christopher, 1969–    author.
Title: Fear itself : the causes and consequences of fear in america / Christopher D. Bader, Joseph O. Baker, L. Edward Day, and Ann Gordon.
Description: New York : NYU Press, 2020. | Includes bibliographical references and index.
Identifiers: LCCN 2019006870 | ISBN 9781479864362 (cl : alk. paper) | ISBN 9781479869817 (pb : alk. paper)
Subjects: LCSH: Fear—United States. | United States—Social conditions—21st century. | United States—Politics and government—21st century.
Classification: LCC BF575.F2 F434 2020 | DDC 152.4/6—dc23
LC record available at https://lccn.loc.gov/2019006870

New York University Press books are printed on acid-free paper, and their binding materials are chosen for strength and durability. We strive to use environmentally responsible suppliers and materials to the greatest extent possible in publishing our books.

Manufactured in the United States of America

10 9 8 7 6 5 4 3 2 1

Also available as an ebook

*Dedication*

*You know who you are.*

# CONTENTS

# FOREWORD

EARL BABBIE

At first, the study of fear seems a narrowly specific topic for research, but it soon becomes apparent that fear is metastasized throughout many of the volatile issues that shape individual and societal life. This book, drawing on and analyzing the annual Chapman University Survey of American Fears, provides an in-depth and broad-ranging examination of what worries Americans most. And it's not what you might think.

Ghosts, zombies, terrorism, and robbery don't even make the top 10. After 242 years of a democratic experiment, Americans are most likely to choose "corruption of government officials" as something they fear. Perhaps this should come as no surprise. In the news during the last few years, some of the biggest stories have concerned members of Donald Trump's presidential campaign and presidential administration being convicted or pleading guilty to a variety of crimes. Several cabinet members have been charged with ethics violations, and Tom Price and Scott Pruitt were driven from office.

Such scandals did not begin with Donald Trump, however. There are countless examples throughout American history. Watergate and Teapot Dome come to mind. Nor is the pattern of public corruption limited to national politics. Four of the past seven Illinois governors have moved from the State House to the Big House, serving time in prison: three Democrats and one Republican. Corruption is a bipartisan pastime.

The advantage of a longitudinal study like the one on which this book draws is the opportunity to observe changes in American fears over time. For example, in 2018 the fear selected by most respondents (73.6 percent) was "the corruption of government officials," as noted earlier. That was also the leading fear in the 2017 survey, selected by roughly the same percentage (74.5 percent). While it was also the leading fear in the 2016 survey, a substantially lower percentage selected it (60.6 percent). It is interesting that this increase occurred during the period that American intelligence services now tell us that Russian trolls on Internet media were not only promoting the candidacy of Donald Trump but were even more interested in sowing distrust of government among American citizens.

The long list of phenomena that Americans fear is only the beginning, however. This book's analysis examines who is the most afraid and why. As you might imagine, anxiety, paranoia, and phobias are commonly accompanied by a long list of fears, although the direction of causation is uncertain.

One of the more interesting discoveries lies in the connection between fears and the belief in conspiracy theories. Many Americans have become convinced that we have not been told the "truth" about such events as 9/11, the Kennedy assassination, the moon landing, Area 51, and on it goes. Alex Jones has convinced some Americans that the Sandy Hook school shooting was made up and that no children actually died. (He is currently being sued by the parents of some of the young victims.)

The most unsettling finding for me was the discovery that a third of the sample believed there was a cover-up regarding the South Dakota crash. You may be unfamiliar with that event since the researchers made it up. There was no "South Dakota crash," but one American in three believes there was a cover-up. That discovery put a new fear at the top of my list: a fear of people who believe such things.

By the time you complete this book, you will be amazed by this unusual aspect of American life. Be clear, many things are worthy of our fears. For example, the fear of environmental degradation is high on the list for the Americans sampled in this study. The authors of this book do not intend to dismiss fears altogether. However, they demonstrate the many ways in which some fears can paralyze us and distract us from things actually worth fearing.

Clearly, I have the highest regard for this book, and my assessment is unbiased by the fact that the annual Chapman University Survey of American Fears from which it emerges was a project of the Earl Babbie Research Center. Just a coincidence, perhaps. The book is well worth your time and attention in any event.

Earl Babbie
Campbell Professor of Behavioral Science (Emeritus)
Chapman University

# Introduction

On July 1, 2015, Kathryn Steinle was enjoying a walk along Pier 14 with her father and a friend. It was a beautiful day with friends and family, a day without fear.

Then Jim Steinle heard a loud bang. His 32-year-old daughter slumped against him; said, "Help me, Dad";[1] and collapsed onto the concrete pier. Searching frantically for what was wrong, he found a bullet hole in his daughter's back. He began CPR. Paramedics arrived quickly. Two hours later, Kathryn Steinle was declared dead at San Francisco General Hospital. The bullet had pierced her aorta.[2]

The shot that killed Kathryn had been fired by Jose Inez García Zárate, an undocumented immigrant under the influence of sleeping pills he claimed to have found in the garbage. García Zárate had been deported from the United States five times and had a criminal record with several felonies, including drug charges and illegal attempts at border crossing. Having been recently caught attempting to cross the border in Texas again, García Zárate was passed around the justice system and, by March 2015, sat in jail in San Francisco awaiting a decade-old felony charge of possessing and selling marijuana.

Further heightening the tragic circumstances behind the case, U.S. Immigration and Customs Enforcement (ICE) had requested that García Zárate be held until he could be deported once again. But he was released from the San Francisco jail on April 15, 2015, after prosecutors dropped the marijuana charges.

Media outlets made the shooting into a national story, a morality tale on the dangers of illegal immigration, in the run-up to a presidential election.[3] While some headlines focused on the grief ("Family Devastated After Woman Shot, Killed in San Francisco"),[4] many turned to finding blame in local policies. Among the headlines were "San Francisco Jailers Dumped a Prisoner and Kathryn Steinle Died,"[5] "How San Francisco Aided and Abetted the Murder of Kate Steinle,"[6] and "Murderer: I Chose

SF Because It Is A 'Sanctuary City.'"[7] Politicians on both sides of the aisle criticized the decisions that led to Zárate's release. Then-candidate Donald Trump featured the case in his Twitter feed and speeches. Both houses of Congress saw bills to create stiffer sentences for those illegally entering the country and to punish jurisdictions with sanctuary laws. When a jury acquitted the immigrant of all murder charges, a second round of anti-immigrant fervor was ignited.[8]

Part of the reason that Steinle's shooting became a cultural touchstone was that it simultaneously tapped into a number of America's greatest fears—guns, drugs, random acts of violence, illegal immigrants, and a justice system that seems to prioritize "criminals" over law-abiding citizens. But this simple story of a hardened "criminal alien" preying on the innocent was, in fact, far more complicated than it first appeared.[9]

First, as opposed to being a random, predatory attack, it is highly probable that Steinle's shooting was accidental, as García Zárate testified at the trial (although he initially told police he was shooting at a sea lion). The bullet had ricocheted off the concrete pier some 12 to 15 feet in front of García Zárate before hitting the victim another 80 to 90 feet away. As one ballistics expert noted, "You couldn't do this on purpose."[10] The jury members agreed that the shooting was accidental or, at least, had reasonable doubt. They found García Zárate not guilty of first-degree murder, second-degree murder, and involuntary manslaughter, convicting him only of being a felon in possession of a firearm.

García Zárate claimed that he had found the gun only moments before the shooting, wrapped in cloth underneath the bench where he was sitting. During the investigation, it emerged that the weapon, a .40-caliber Sig Sauer P239, actually belonged to a ranger with the U.S. Bureau of Land Management (BLM). It had been stolen from his sport utility vehicle four days earlier while it was parked on a downtown San Francisco street in a lighted, metered spot. The gun had been inside a backpack, stashed behind the driver's seat with the seat reclined. Someone had smashed a window to gain entry. The ranger testified during García Zárate's trial that he "typically" carried his weapon with him, in the backpack, to protect his family. A BLM investigation determined that the ranger did not violate agency policies on the storing of weapons.[11] That policy has since been changed.

García Zárate's release from jail shortly before the incident was also not the simple case of bureaucratic bungling that it appeared to be. San Francisco operates as a "sanctuary city" and does not cooperate with ICE on cases that do not involve violent felony charges. Not only was García Zárate being held for nonviolent drug charges; none of his previous convictions were for violent offenses either. Long ago, San Francisco prosecutors had deprioritized nonviolent marijuana cases in their heavy caseloads. And, as in many cities, local officials feared that cooperation with federal immigration enforcement would diminish their ability to control local crime by making immigrant victims and witnesses afraid to cooperate with local police.

So the shooting and death of Kate Steinle are complicated, to say the least. What *is* clear is that none of the heightened, politically motivated responses from the left and the right would actually reduce the likelihood that such an event could happen in the future. It remains unclear whether García Zárate stole the weapon himself or found the stolen gun. Either way, it is unlikely that stiffer gun control legislation, such as improved background checks or longer waiting periods, would have kept the weapon out of his hands. Tougher laws to ensure that violent criminals are kept off the streets would not have prevented the incident because García Zárate had only nonviolent offenses on his record. And forcing cities such as San Francisco to hold nonviolent offenders for ICE could serve to increase crime overall, should doing so break down lines of communication between police officers and immigrant communities. Of course, the most obvious and frequently politicized "solution" to cases such as García Zárate's would be to curb illegal immigration, but that, too, would have a dubious effect at best. An abundance of recent research has demonstrated that communities with higher percentages of immigrants have lower crime rates, including lower homicide rates,[12] and that immigrants tend to commit fewer crimes than native-born Americans.[13] None of these responses would have addressed the complex, underlying causes of crime and violence or why immigrants try to come to the United States in the first place. And no proposals addressed the deeply personal tragedy and grief suffered by the Steinle family. As Kathryn Steinle's mother said, "Everybody is trying to put the political spin on it. But it happened, and there is no taking it back."[14]

## Fear Itself

Ultimately, incidents such as the tragic Steinle shooting can have dramatic impacts on politics, laws, and the criminal justice system, whether or not those changes will *actually* help. For example, the fear generated by such cases may, indeed, result in more restrictive immigration policies, but these are unlikely to cause a decrease in crime rates.

Social scientists have long observed that the merits of the claims underlying a fear or panic are far less important than the influence those fears have on other beliefs and behaviors. Sociologist W. I. Thomas famously observed, "If [people] define situations as real, they are real in their consequences."[15]

The consequences are manifold, for the United States has become a culture driven by fear.[16] Fear negatively impacts decision-making abilities,[17] pushes people to vote for certain candidates in elections,[18] and causes anxiety, depression, and reduced physical health,[19] as well as social isolation[20] and the decay of our communities as individuals retreat from public spaces.[21] Others take advantage of those fears. Politicians generate and use fear to garner votes and gather support for legislation.[22] Companies market unnecessary products to consumers promising protection from exaggerated harms.[23] And fear-driven decisions often make things worse. People who travel by car because they are afraid to fly are taking a much riskier form of transportation and increase mortality rates due to accidents. Citizens afraid to relax in public parks leave these spaces more open to criminal behavior. And a gun carried to protect one's family can inadvertently end up being used to kill an innocent young woman walking with her father.

Despite countless ill effects on the well-being of society and a substantial literature in psychology,[24] the study and understanding of fear remain underdeveloped.[25] A number of scholars have called for a reexamination of the impact of fear on society, with eminent Hungarian sociologist Elemér Hankiss lamenting that fear is "much neglected in the social sciences."[26] In the hopes of better understanding the prevalence of fear and its relation to other aspects of social life, we undertook a unique, multiyear examination of Americans' greatest fears.

## The Study of Fear

In one sense, we all know what fear is. We have all experienced situations where we were afraid of something. Everyone can recall frightening experiences that left a deep impression in our memories. But this does not mean that fear is simple, monolithic, or experienced the same by different people. Furthermore, distinguishing subjective experiences of fear from their underlying neural processes is critical. Regarding the latter, scientific understanding about the physiological pathways and evolutionary aspects of fear has increased rapidly in recent years thanks to advances in neuroimaging and experiments with other mammals.[27]

Neuroscientist Joseph LeDoux, a leading expert on the biological underpinnings of the threat detection and defense processes of the human brain, stresses that, while clearly interconnected, the biological processes of threat detection and the subjective experience of fear are distinct and must be conceptualized accordingly. Thus, while "fear is the most extensively studied emotion," we know more about its underlying physiological dimensions than we do about the range and patterns of subjective experiences of fear among general populations.[28] Although scientists have begun to identify the physiological and cognitive aspects involved in threat detection, understanding subjective fear must incorporate a wider range of considerations, including social identity, situational contexts, and biographical and experiential factors.[29] Consequently, "The experience of fear, the conscious emotional feeling we propose, results when a first-order representation of the threat enters into a [higher-order representation], along with relevant long-term memories—including emotion schema—that are retrieved."[30]

So to study fear itself, rather than its underlying physiological dimensions, we need systematic and wide-ranging self-report data on experiences of fear. Fear is a conscious state, and "verbal self-report remains the gold standard in studies of consciousness."[31] In this sense, we hope to fill in an important but understudied aspect of fear by empirically examining self-reports of fear among the general population across a wide range of fear domains. That is, where neuroscience has advanced our understanding of the biological dimensions of fear, our goal is to advance the social psychological, sociological, and political understanding of fear among Americans in the early twenty-first century. After undertaking this endeavor, we will return to the physiological and cognitive dimensions of fear, connecting the neuroscience of fear to the social patterns we identify among the public, to advance a more holistic understanding of fear and its myriad accompanying personal and social consequences.

Fear is a perennial topic for surveys and polls. In October 2017 alone we learned that 72 percent of Americans feared that the United States would soon become embroiled in a major war (*Newsweek*),[32] 70 percent feared robots taking jobs from humans (Pew Research Center),[33] 4 in 10 feared being the victim of a mass shooting (Gallup),[34] 43 percent were too afraid to purchase a home with a reputation for hauntings (Trulia),[35] and one third feared walking alone near their home at night (also Gallup).[36] Simply put, whenever a new crisis or horrific crime hits the news, or when Halloween or a Friday the 13th approaches, we can expect a poll documenting how many Americans are fearful of some particular thing. Although such polls can be entertaining and even sometimes educational, they produce little in terms of a deeper understanding of the role of fear in American life. They are singular snapshots. What we need is a photo album.

In 2014, we attempted to fill the gap in the social scientific understanding of fear by undertaking an unprecedented study. With the help of an interdisciplinary group of researchers affiliated with the Earl Babbie Research Center at Chapman University, we developed the Chapman University Survey of American Fears (CSAF). For five years we administered an annual survey to a random sample of Americans.[37] Our surveys include the largest set of items ever asked about fear. We asked Americans how afraid they are of crime (in many forms), terrorism, and different types of natural disasters. We found out who is afraid of running out of money, getting sick, losing their jobs, or dying. Our respondents told us how afraid they were of illegal immigration, government corruption, and mass shootings. We even learned about specific phobias by asking Americans if they are afraid of heights, reptiles, spiders, needles, public speaking, and a host of other (potentially) frightening things. From air pollution to zombies, we know more about Americans' fears than ever before.[38]

## Americans' Fears

Indeed, Americans are afraid of many things. Our latest survey asked a nationally representative sample of Americans to indicate how afraid they are of over 90 different phenomena, with the possible responses of "very afraid," "afraid," "slightly afraid," or "not afraid at all." Table I.1 provides a complete list of these fears, ordered by the highest percentage of Americans who report being either "very afraid" or "afraid" of each.

The 2018 list of fears reflects political unrest and uncertainty following Donald Trump's election as president. In the wake of a contentious political campaign in which both sides accused the other of being corrupt, it is not surprising that the majority of Americans, about three quarters, were afraid of corrupt government officials, a sign of the divisive nature of American politics. Trump's early promises to make sweeping changes to the U.S. health care system likely stoked fears about health, with more than half of Americans reporting fear of high medical bills (53 percent) and people they love becoming ill (57 percent) or dying (57 percent). Economic concerns, a perennial source of fear, were also felt by the majority of Americans, with 57 percent fearing they will not have enough money for the future.

After his election, Trump spoke openly about withdrawing from the Paris Climate Accords as soon as possible (2020). The Trump administration had also ordered the U.S. Environmental Protection Agency (EPA) not to enforce major pollution laws and fired the EPA's entire Science Advisory Board. These actions appear to have heightened concerns about the environment. Five of the top 10 fears of 2018 related to the environment, including fearing the pollution of oceans, rivers, and lakes (62 percent); the pollution of drinking water (61 percent); air pollution (55 percent); the extinction of plant and animal species (54 percent); and global warming/climate change (53 percent).

Compare this to a list of the top 10 fears from our 2016 survey (see Table I.2), in which fears about the environment did not appear.

This suggests that some fears or elevation in those fears are responses to current events. Other fears appear to be more consistent. The fear of corrupt government officials was the most commonly held fear in our surveys in 2015, 2016, 2017, and 2018. This tells us that the high level of fear among Americans of corrupt government officials is not

TABLE I.1. American Fears 2018.

| Sorted by percentage afraid | Percentage afraid or very afraid |
|---|---|
| 1. Corrupt government officials | 73.6 |
| 2. Pollution of oceans, rivers, and lakes | 61.6 |
| 3. Pollution of drinking water | 60.7 |
| 4. Not having enough money for the future | 57 |
| 5. People I love becoming seriously ill | 56.5 |
| 6. People I love dying | 56.4 |
| 7. Air pollution | 55.1 |
| 8. Extinction of plant and animal species | 54.1 |
| 9. Global warming and climate change | 53.2 |
| 10. High medical bills | 52.9 |
| 11. Cyber-terrorism | 52.5 |
| 12. The U.S. will be involved in another world war | 51.6 |
| 13. Islamic extremists | 49.3 |
| 14. White supremacists | 49.3 |
| 15. Economic/financial collapse | 49.2 |
| 16. Identity theft | 46.6 |
| 17. Corporate tracking of personal data | 46.3 |
| 18. Government tracking of personal data | 46 |
| 19. Being hit by a drunk driver | 45.3 |
| 20. Biological warfare | 44.7 |
| 21. Becoming seriously ill | 44.1 |
| 22. Oil spills | 44 |
| 23. Terrorist attack | 43.8 |
| 24. Widespread civil unrest | 43 |
| 25. Nuclear weapons attack | 42.9 |
| 26. Credit card fraud | 42.6 |
| 27. Extreme anti-immigration groups | 41.6 |
| 28. Random mass shooting | 41.5 |
| 29. Terrorism | 39.8 |
| 30. North Korea using nuclear weapons | 39.2 |
| 31. The collapse of the electrical grid | 39 |
| 32. Pandemic or a major epidemic | 38.6 |
| 33. Government restrictions on firearms and ammunition | 37.8 |
| 34. Devastating drought | 37.7 |

TABLE I.1. (*cont.*)

| Sorted by percentage afraid | Percentage afraid or very afraid |
|---|---|
| 35. Iran using nuclear weapons | 36.4 |
| 36. Losing my data, photos, or other important documents in a disaster | 36.3 |
| 37. Nuclear accident/meltdown | 36 |
| 38. Break-ins | 35.1 |
| 39. Devastating tornado | 34.7 |
| 40. Being unemployed | 34.4 |
| 41. Heights | 33.6 |
| 42. Theft of property | 33.3 |
| 43. Devastating hurricane | 32.8 |
| 44. Government use of drones within the U.S. | 32.3 |
| 45. Militia/patriot movement | 31.3 |
| 46. Devastating flood | 31.1 |
| 47. Devastating earthquake | 30.9 |
| 48. Computers replacing people in the workforce | 30.7 |
| 49. Devastating wildfire | 30.7 |
| 50. Murder by a stranger | 29.7 |
| 51. Sharks | 29.2 |
| 52. Mugging | 28.6 |
| 53. Racial/hate crime | 28.6 |
| 54. Dying | 27.9 |
| 55. Gang violence | 27.8 |
| 56. Financial fraud (such as a Ponzi scheme, embezzlement, etc.) | 27.2 |
| 57. Sexual assault by a stranger | 27.1 |
| 58. Devastating blizzard/winter storm | 27 |
| 59. Police brutality | 26.6 |
| 60. Public speaking | 26.2 |
| 61. Deep lakes and oceans | 25.7 |
| 62. Abduction/kidnapping | 25.1 |
| 63. Reptiles (snakes, lizards, etc.) | 24.1 |
| 64. Stalking | 23.7 |
| 65. Hell | 23.7 |
| 66. Walking alone at night | 23.5 |
| 67. The devil/Satan | 23.1 |
| 68. Insects/arachnids (spiders, bees, etc.) | 22.6 |

TABLE I.1. (*cont.*)

| Sorted by percentage afraid | Percentage afraid or very afraid |
|---|---|
| 69. Illegal immigration | 21.5 |
| 70. Murder by someone you know | 21 |
| 71. Demons | 20.8 |
| 72. Antifa | 20.7 |
| 73. Small enclosed spaces | 19.8 |
| 74. Sexual assault by someone you know | 19.2 |
| 75. Large volcanic eruption | 18.6 |
| 76. Technology I don't understand | 17.8 |
| 77. Being fooled by "fake" news | 17.5 |
| 78. Extreme environmentalists | 16.4 |
| 79. Apocalypse/Armageddon | 16.4 |
| 80. God | 14.2 |
| 81. Germs | 13.2 |
| 82. Needles | 12.9 |
| 83. Flying | 12.7 |
| 84. Significant other cheating on you | 12.1 |
| 85. Extreme animal rightists | 11.3 |
| 86. Sharing a restroom with a transgender person | 9.5 |
| 87. Whites no longer being the majority in the U.S. | 9.4 |
| 88. Zombies | 8.4 |
| 89. Ghosts | 8.3 |
| 90. Sexual harassment in the workplace | 7.5 |
| 91. Clowns | 7.1 |
| 92. Strangers | 7 |
| 93. Others talking about you behind your back | 6.7 |
| 94. Blood | 6.3 |
| 95. Animals (dogs, rats, etc.) | 3.7 |

just a response to Trump. Indeed, his campaign capitalized on this fear and distrust of the political system. On the other hand, only 58 percent of Americans feared corrupt government officials in 2015, compared to 74 percent as of 2018. Our ability to chart fear over time will help us learn which fears are mostly reflections of current events and

TABLE I.2. Top 10 Fears of Americans (2016).

| Top 10 Fears of 2016 | Percentage Afraid or Very Afraid |
|---|---|
| Corrupt government officials | 60.6 |
| Terrorist attack | 41 |
| Not having enough money for the future | 39.9 |
| Terrorism | 38.5 |
| Government restrictions on firearms and ammunition | 38.5 |
| People I love dying | 38.1 |
| Economic/financial collapse | 37.5 |
| Identity theft | 37.1 |
| People I love becoming seriously ill | 35.9 |
| The Affordable Health Care Act/Obamacare | 35.5 |

circumstances and which seem to be continual sources of worry but are not subject to fluctuations dependent on the administration in power or the events of the day.

## The Road Ahead

While examining changes in the percentage of Americans reporting a certain fear can be useful, this is not the most important part of studying fear. Rather, our goal is to understand the patterns and consequences of fear. We seek to understand what kinds of Americans are afraid of certain things and how those fears are related to other beliefs and behaviors. To do so, our surveys also asked respondents a broad series of questions regarding potential causes of fear, such as anxiety, media consumption patterns, and neighborhood characteristics. We also asked about potential outcomes of fear, such as the purchasing of guns and other forms of personal protection, preparation for natural disasters, avoidance of public settings, and other behavioral changes and beliefs that may be related to fear, such as belief in conspiracy theories or the belief that the world is becoming more dangerous. Throughout this book, we explore the many social and political implications of fear across a wide variety of domains, from the fear of crime to the belief in 9/11 conspiracies, responses to natural disasters, and most everything in between.

Our goal is to spur both further research and a greater understanding of fear and its effects. To those ends, we have written this book with a broader readership in mind. When we discuss our many analyses, we present simplified results. Those readers who wish to dive into the complicated details of the analyses driving each chapter can find the necessary tables at http://www.theArda.com/Fear. Here you will also find links for downloading the actual data sets should you wish to explore fear further on your own.

This book *is* about fear and its potentially disastrous social and political consequences, but we are not helpless in its wake. After our examination of some of the many consequences of fear, we end this book by reminding readers of the many ways that you can manage fear and actively change your communities for the better by resisting its lure.

1

The Sum of All Fears

In December 2014, someone with the measles visited Disneyland. As reported by the Centers for Disease Control and Prevention (CDC), this infected tourist, likely from overseas, coughed or sneezed while strolling the park and exposed other vacationers and park employees to the virus. Normally, exposure to measles would not be problematic, as the MMR (measles, mumps, and rubella) vaccine is widely available in the United States. But in recent years, fear had developed among certain segments of the population that vaccinations can cause autism, stoked by the very public anti-vaccination campaign of actress Jenny McCarthy. During a 2007 appearance on Oprah Winfrey's talk show, McCarthy espoused the belief that her son's autism was caused by the MMR vaccine and peddled her book *Louder Than Words: A Mother's Journey in Healing Autism*. Coverage of McCarthy and the claims of other "anti-vaxxers" was successful in creating skepticism about the benefits of vaccines. The CDC estimates as few as 50 percent of those exposed to the Disneyland virus had been vaccinated.

In the second wave of our survey of American fears (2015), we included a series of items designed to gauge Americans' opinions about vaccination. We asked Americans if vaccines can cause autism, if "drug companies aren't being honest about the risks from vaccinations," and if, these days, American children "get too many vaccinations," all common claims of the anti-vaccination movement.[1] Distrust of what drug companies are saying about vaccinations was quite high, with more than half (52 percent) of Americans believing that drug makers are not completely disclosing vaccination risks. Nearly one-fifth of Americans (19 percent) believe there is a connection between vaccines and autism.

Curiously, public discussion about the anti-vaccination movement only served to spread myths about its adherents. In 2017, LiveScience reported that the "vast majority" of people commenting, sharing, and liking anti-vaccination information on Facebook were women.[2] The state of California allows personal belief exemptions from vaccination. The *Los Angeles Times* found that these exemptions were used most often in "wealthy coastal and mountain communities,"[3] and particularly in private schools, leading the paper to conclude that "rich, educated and stupid parents are driving the vaccination crisis."[4] The reader could be forgiven from drawing the conclusion from such coverage that the typical anti-vaxxer is a highly educated, higher income woman. But such a conclusion would be problematic at best. We can tell little about the actual demographics of anti-vaccination beliefs from Facebook postings. Online usage does not represent a random sample of Americans. Besides, women are more likely than men to use Facebook.[5] Likewise, the fact that private schools see more claimed exemptions from vaccinations does not necessarily mean that higher-income individuals are more likely to hold anti-vaccination beliefs. The income relationship could be a simple function of the nature of private schools; after all, they tend to be expensive and may have characteristics (such as a religious orientation) that are associated with skepticism about vaccinations.

If we want to combat unnecessary fears based on false information, we cannot begin that quest with false information. With this purpose, we started the Chapman University Survey of American Fears (CSAF): to document what Americans fear and to understand both the characteristics of those who fear and the consequences of those fears for people's lives. Every year we survey a new, random sample of Americans. These samples are representative of the general population, meaning that, unlike the online convenience polls we hear so much about, we can confidently make assertions that our findings represent the current state of beliefs and fears among Americans. Our findings can show us who *really* believes that vaccines are dangerous.

To determine patterns of anti-vaccination, we created a scale that added responses to the six questions we asked respondents about vaccinations.[6] Possible scores ranged from 0 to 18. A person who received a zero on our Anti-Vaxx scale has rejected entirely the claims of the movement, strongly disagreeing that there is a link between vaccines and autism, that parents should be allowed to choose vaccinations, and so on. An individual who scored an 18 on the Anti-Vaxx scale is in complete alignment with Jenny McCarthy and other hardline vaccine skeptics, believing that children receive too many vaccinations, which provide little benefit and may cause autism.

The idea that the anti-vaccination movement was largely composed of elites makes good copy but simply does not match reality. It is a common mistake to assume that the most visible faces of a moral crusade are representative of its membership. Sociologists have long known that the leaders of movements that produce exaggerated claims about the dangers of a product or group of people are "dominated by those in the upper levels of the social structure" and not typically reflective of those who become convinced by their claims.[7] After all, societal elites have greater access to the resources that will allow them to promote their claims publicly.

We performed a multivariate analysis that allows us to determine how a host of personal characteristics are associated with anti-vaccination beliefs while controlling for other related factors. We examined gender, education, income, race/ethnicity, region of the country, whether or not the respondent lives in a metro area, employment status, political conservatism and political party, and multiple indicators of religiosity.[8] The average American exhibits some skepticism about vaccines, scoring a 7 on our Anti-Vaxx scale. But such beliefs precipitously decline with education. On average, a person with no formal education scores an 11 (out of 18) on our scale of anti-vaccination beliefs. Those who have achieved a bachelor's degree are far less conspiratorial about vaccines, scoring a 6 on our scale, and those with a PhD score only 5. Income is also significantly and negatively related to anti-vaccination beliefs, with those earning less than $7,500 a year having the highest Anti-Vaxx scores and those earning $175,000 a year or more the lowest. Controlling for all these factors, gender had no effect on anti-vaccination beliefs. Men were just as likely to be skeptical about vaccines as women.

All told, the person most likely to hold anti-vaccination beliefs is a younger, politically conservative, nonwhite person of either gender who has a lower level of income and education. The problem of anti-vaccination is not an issue of too much education but, rather, too little. To combat such beliefs, policy makers will need to invest more heavily in public education, particularly science-based public education.

\*\*\*

Ultimately, 145 people in the United States and dozens more in Canada and Mexico contracted measles from "patient x's" visit to Disneyland in 2014.[9] It could have been much worse. By April, no new cases had been reported, and no one had died from their exposure. Yet the incident highlights the key role fears play in American society. We often find ourselves in crises of our own making, situations simultaneously created and exacerbated by our fears. The first step in addressing some of the social problems caused by fear is a clear understanding of *who* fears *what* and *why* based on high-quality data.

## Fear Factors

Our surveys asked Americans about dozens of specific fears, ranging from fear of sharks to nuclear attacks and running out of money. Exploring the demographic patterns behind each of these fears individually would be unnecessarily tedious; however, many of these specific fears are about similar underlying concepts. For instance, we asked respondents how much they fear the pollution of drinking water, the pollution of oceans and lakes, the extinction of plants and animals, oil spills, and global warming. Although it is certainly possible that some individuals, because of where they live or life circumstances, might fear the pollution of their drinking water but have little concern about the other items, for most respondents, views on these issues are likely to be closely related. Someone fearful about oil spills probably worries about ocean pollution too. We used factor analysis to look for such patterns in our data.[10] If respondents answered in a similar way to a selection of items, factor analysis will group them together. Our analysis determined that the myriad of fears could be collapsed into 11 major "fear factors" (see Table 1.1), ranging from the fear of crime and victimization to the fear of technology, as well as fears about sharks, clowns, ghosts, and other animals/entities.

## Divided by Fear

Fears often reflect social and political divisions. To find out who was more likely to be afraid of different types of phenomena, we conducted an in-depth series of analyses. We determined how our fear factors

TABLE 1.1. Fear Factors.

| Fear factor | Includes fears of . . . |
|---|---|
| Animals/Entities | Insects, reptiles, animals, sharks, germs, clowns, ghosts, zombies, strangers |
| Crime/ Victimization | Walking alone at night, mugging, stalking, murder by a stranger, murder by someone you know, being a victim of a drunk driver, police brutality, sexual assault by a stranger, sexual assault by someone you know, hate crime, mass shootings, break-ins, theft, gang violence, kidnapping, financial fraud, being the victim of terrorism |
| Environmental | Air pollution, pollution of drinking water, pollution of the oceans, extinction of plant and animal species, oil spills, global warming |
| Government | Corrupt government officials, government tracking of personal information, government use of drones |
| Man-made disasters | Electromagnetic pulse attack, nuclear attack, nuclear meltdown, economic collapse, pandemics, widespread civil unrest, world war, biological warfare, terrorist attacks, North Korea using nuclear weapons |
| Natural Disasters | Earthquakes, hurricanes, tornadoes, floods, blizzards, droughts, volcanoes |
| Personal tragedies | Becoming ill, loved ones becoming ill, dying, loved ones dying, high medical bills, becoming unemployed, running out of money, others talking about me |
| Phobias | Blood, needles, flying, heights, public speaking, small spaces, water |
| Technology | Being fooled by fake news, computers replacing the workforce, technology I don't understand, cybercrime, corporate tracking of personal information, identity theft, credit card theft, losing personal data |
| Things American conservatives fear | Islamic extremists, extreme animal rights groups, extreme environmental groups, left-wing extremists, whites no longer being the majority, illegal immigrants, gun control, Obamacare |
| Things American liberals fear | Sovereign citizens, militias, white supremacists, anti-immigration groups, anti-abortion groups, anti-tax groups, Trumpcare |

varied by gender, race/ethnicity, and age. We looked at how fears varied by education, marital status, employment, and income and tested for the possibility that levels of fear differ by region of the country or whether people lived in a rural or a metro area. Religion is an important aspect of cultural frameworks about right and wrong and, therefore, also what should be feared (or not). We examined the effects of religion by looking at patterns based on religious identity, how frequently people attend religious services (if at all), and whether people think of themselves as biblical "literalists."[11]

We also asked respondents about their political orientation on a 7-point scale ranging from "extremely liberal" to "extremely conservative" with "moderate" in the middle.[12] Political orientation had little effect on most of the fears we included in our surveys. But some specific items clearly tapped into the concerns of either liberals or conservatives, and for these issues, the effects of politics were quite pronounced.

For example, fears of Islamic extremists, extreme animal-rights groups, extreme environmental groups, left-wing extremists, whites losing majority status, gun control, and Obamacare clustered together. In other words, it is a safe bet that someone who expresses a high level of fear about Obamacare is also quite afraid of gun control. The following list provides those personal characteristics that were significantly related to higher levels of conservative fear. The effects presented are standardized, meaning they can be compared to one another to assess the relative magnitude of effects. Six factors predicted whether a person is afraid of Obamacare, Islamic extremists, and other conservative concerns, in ascending order by their effect size:

- Women (.061)
- Race other than black (.081)
- Biblical literalist (.091)
- Lives in a rural area (.107)
- Older (.154)
- Identifies as conservative (.540)

So, women were more likely to express fears about conservative political issues. African Americans exhibit far lower levels of conservative fear than other racial/ethnic groups.[13] Both effects were smaller than that of being a biblical literalist or living in a rural area, which were themselves smaller effects than that of being older. But dwarfing all those effects was describing oneself as conservative. The effect of being a self-identified conservative was 3.5 times larger than the next largest factor (being older).

When it comes to things liberals tend to fear, including fear of Trumpcare, white supremacists, militias, sovereign citizens, anti-abortion groups, anti-immigration groups, and anti-tax groups, we find a different profile:

- Older (.091)
- Black (.116)

- Hispanic (.135)
- Religion reported as "just Christian" (−.183)
- Religion reported as Catholic (−.204)
- Religion reported as Protestant (−.227)
- Identifies as liberal (.362)

As with conservative fears, one's political orientation has, by far, the biggest effect on being fearful about "liberal issues." Similar to what we find for conservative fears, older people tend to be more fearful. From here, the profile differs significantly. Nonwhites, specifically Hispanics and African Americans, express more fear about liberal political issues. Negative numbers indicate that a group is *less* fearful than others. Those who self-identify as Christians, whether that be as a Protestant, a Catholic, or "just Christian," are much less frightened than people who hold a non-Christian identity (religions other than Christianity, the nonreligious, and atheists).

\*\*\*

These profiles of conservatives and liberals are not surprising. What *did* prove quite shocking to us was how sharply the political divide in the United States is expressed via our fears (see Figure 1.1). It is not that conservatives and liberals have different ideas about how to fix the issues that cause them anxiety and fear. They simply do not fear the same things at all, and that itself is frightening.

Politicians and political consultants have long known that fear serves as a mobilizing force.[14] As political scientists have demonstrated, emotions play a key role in voters' attention to politics, decision making, and participation.[15] There are two general sets of processes in the brain. The first, known as the disposition system, addresses long-term habits of mind and is associated with decision making that relies on deeply ingrained values and identity, including partisanship and ideology. By contrast, the surveillance system is engaged when voters encounter new and especially frightening circumstances or information. We might think of this as the "fight or flight" reaction. It captures one's attention and corresponds to anxiety and fear. It leads to greater information seeking behaviors. Thus, nuanced, reasoned arguments outlining differences of opinion on a political issue are simultaneously resistant to

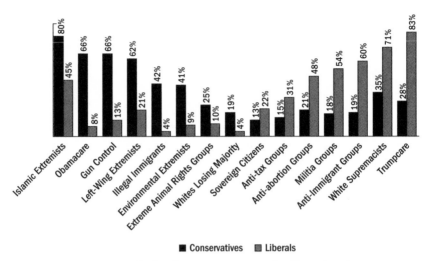

Figure 1.1. Conservative and Liberal Fears: Percentage Afraid by Political Orientation (2017).

being sound bites and less likely to garner attention and persuade voters, whereas appeals to fear activate the surveillance system and therefore cue attentiveness.[16]

Perhaps the most infamous fear appeal in a presidential campaign was the Daisy Girl advertisement. In this 60-second spot, a young girl is innocently picking petals off a daisy. Her counting gradually becomes a threatening voice-over of a nuclear launch countdown and ends with a terrifying mushroom cloud. President Lyndon Johnson grabbed voters' attention by activating the surveillance system and pushing the message that Barry Goldwater was a threat to peace and stability. More than 40 years later, Hillary Clinton's spot "3 AM" opens with sleeping children and a narrator reminding the viewer that it's a dangerous world. The ad poses the question of who should pick up the phone in the White House at 3 AM in a crisis: "Your vote will decide who will answer that call . . . who do you want answering the phone?"[17] The message is clear that Clinton's experience and level-headed leadership is the safe choice.

Real-world events also trigger the surveillance system and lead to changes in political behavior. For example, fear of terrorism has an impact on voter turnout and decisions. Voter turnout rates in U.S. urban areas are affected by terrorist attacks, with higher rates of turnout occurring with an increased frequency and severity of attacks.[18]

Although fear is part of the surveillance system and partisan decision making is located within the disposition system, we have found evidence that particular fears are linked to partisan predispositions. A strong relationship between political orientation and fear could mean different things. It is possible that politicians have been successful in creating fear or, at least, piggybacking on shocking or terrifying events to tailor messages that simultaneously appeal to partisans and activate their surveillance systems. By discussing tragic (but rare) cases of crimes perpetrated by undocumented immigrants, conservative politicians have heightened fear of immigrants in general, priming the electorate to use this issue as the basis for candidate evaluations.[19] Similarly, a liberal politician, knowing that potential voters are very frightened of white supremacists, might highlight recent violent acts committed by racist groups, leading those who hear those messages to prioritize voting for a politician whom they feel can protect them from such violence. Thus, a kind of feedback loop occurs whereby people with particular values are more likely to respond to messages that stoke their fears, and politicians amplify those fears by exploiting current events and placing fears at the forefront of their campaigns. By campaigning on fear-inducing topics and invoking current events already in the press, heavy media coverage of such themes is ensured. Hearing those messages reported in the media, in turn, (re)activates voters' surveillance systems, reinforces fears, and makes voters more susceptible to future fear-baiting messaging.

Despite the nature of the chicken-and-egg relationship between political orientation and fear, what is *quite clear* is that political fear is strongly related to the media people consume.

Fear TV

People born in the 1990s or later do not remember a time when news and entertainment came from a handful of television stations and, perhaps, local and national newspapers and magazines. The widespread availability of cable television increased the number of available

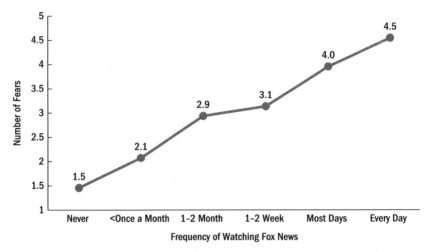

Figure 1.2. Number of Conservative Fears by Frequency of Watching Fox News (2017).

channels and provided the ability to target ever-finer market segments. For example, someone interested in home improvement–related entertainment in the pre-cable era would have had to patiently wait for PBS to show a weekly episode of *This Old House*. Today, multiple cable channels, such as HGTV and the DIY network, are entirely devoted to home improvement. The Internet has further allowed for market segmentation to an unprecedented degree. Information on any topic, no matter how obscure or biased, is immediately available.

Researchers have found important connections between the consumption of media (mostly televised content) and fear, particularly concerning fears about crime and terrorism, issues that we discuss at length in Chapters 4 and 5.[20] Our analyses also showed a very strong relationship between media consumption and fear, but this relationship is greatly dependent on *what* media a person consumes.

Fox News debuted in October 1996, specializing in news with a conservative bent. Scholars have found that frequency of watching Fox News is significantly associated with anti-immigration views,[21] voting for conservative candidates,[22] and skepticism about global warming.[23] We find the same type of relationship (see Figure 1.2). For each respondent, we counted the number of our eight conservative fears (Islamic extremists, extreme animal-rights groups, extreme environmental groups, left-wing extremists, whites losing majority status, illegal immigrants, Obamacare, and gun control) that he or she reported being afraid or very afraid of. A person with a zero is not afraid of any of these things while a person with a score of 8 is frightened of all of them. The more frequently our survey respondents reported watching Fox News, the greater their number of fears related to Obamacare, gun control, illegal immigrants, and other "horrors" frequently addressed by Fox. The effect is quite strong. Someone who reports watching Fox News every day is, on average, afraid of three times as many conservative political concerns compared to someone who never does.

Across the political spectrum from Fox News sits MSNBC, with its well-known progressive hosts such as Chris Matthews and Rachael Maddow. MSNBC viewers are hardly immune from fear; they just fear different things. Fear of Trumpcare, white supremacists, anti-immigrant groups, sovereign citizens, and extreme anti-tax groups steadily increases the more frequently someone watches MSNBC (see Figure 1.3). Those who watch every day are fearful of almost twice as many of these concerns compared to those who never watch MSNBC. Although the effect of MSNBC on liberal fears is less pronounced than the effect of Fox News on conservative fears, that each channel is exacerbating different kinds of fear is evident.

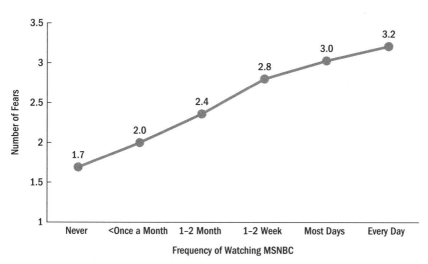

Figure 1.3. Number of Liberal Fears by Frequency of Watching MSNBC (2017).

Given their differing political leanings, it would be natural to view MSNBC and Fox News as in competition with one another and assume that our collective fears will be reflective of whomever "wins." That is mistaken. There will never be a winner.[24] Fox News and MSNBC are not even playing the same game.[25] Everybody wins as long as they can attract a devoted following. Converting the other side's following is not important. The increasing segmentation of the media market into channels, websites, and forums devoted to particular orientations allows consumers to select information that fits their preexisting or nascent political views while almost entirely avoiding alternative information. This phenomenon of information siloing erodes democratic political processes reliant on civic engagement in many ways. One way is by simply making us fear different things and, perhaps, becoming more afraid of one another as a result.

## The Sum of All (Nonpolitical) Fears

The specific fears of liberals and conservatives are different from other types of fear. For *everything else*, the patterns of fear are quite consistent. The types of people who fear reptiles, clowns, and zombies are quite similar to the people who fear tornadoes, earthquakes, and hurricanes. Thus, setting politics aside, we summed all the other nine fear factors to create the "Sum of All Fears." We created standardized scores for each fear factor before adding them together.[26] Therefore, each factor is weighted the same in the scale, regardless of how many items were in the index. Someone with the lowest scores would have far below average levels of fear across the nine nonpolitical fear factors. Someone with the highest level of fear has shown far above average levels of fear across the nine fear factors. Final scores on the Sum of All Fears ranged from 0 (the least fearful people) to 33 (the most fearful people). Of course, most people fell between these two extremes, near the average of 13.1.

\*\*\*

Once we calculated the Sum of All Fears for each person in our survey, we could see which personal characteristics were predictive of overall levels of fear. Our analysis predicted levels of fear using respondents' gender, age, education, income, race/ethnicity, political orientation, previous history of criminal victimization (if any), region of the country, the type of place (metro/nonmetro) in which the person lives, and several indicators of religiosity. Many of these predictors were not significantly related to levels of fear. For example, considering all these factors, fear does not significantly vary by *type* of religion. Protestants were just as frightened as Catholics; Jews were no more or less frightened than atheists. Unlike the political items discussed earlier, political identity had nothing to do with overall levels of fear. Conservatives were no more or less fearful than liberals, controlling for everything else. City dwellers were no different from those who lived in rural areas.

Several personal characteristics were significantly associated with higher levels of fear though. As in our previous analyses, we present standardized coefficients that can be compared for magnitude:

- Education (−.068; higher education equals less fear)
- Lives in the south (.069)
- Unemployed (.086)
- Income (−.115; higher income equals less fear)
- White (−.120; whites less fearful than nonwhites)
- Younger (.175)
- Women (.229)
- Frequency of religious service attendance (.709; curvilinear effect, explained in the following section)

The hypothetical, most frightened person in American is a younger, nonwhite woman who lives somewhere in the South. She has a lower level of education and is likely unemployed, which is, obviously, associated with a lower level of income. But far greater than any of these effects is that of religious service attendance. Here the story becomes more complicated.

## Religion and Fear

The effect of religious service attendance on fear dwarfs all other effects, but it is not a simple relationship where higher levels of attendance equal higher or lower levels of fear. Rather, the effect of religious service attendance on fear is *curvilinear*. What does this mean?

A curvilinear effect is one in which the highest or lowest values for an outcome we are trying to predict are at the mid-levels of the predictor. In this case, we find that people who attend religious services very frequently (more than once a week) have, by far, the lowest average scores on the Sum of All Fears index (9.5). Fear is also comparatively lower among people who *never* attend religious services. Those who never attend score, on average, 12.5 on the Sum of All Fears index. From there fear rises steadily with increasing attendance until it reaches its peak at people who attend "several times a year" (14.6).[27] This curvilinear pattern matches three other well-established curvilinear relationships that researchers have identified regarding religiosity that are highly relevant to understanding the patterns we find with the Sum of All Fears measure.

The first is found when examining levels of religiosity and a specific fear: the fear of death.[28] The highest levels of death fear are found among people with a moderate, rather than a high or low, level of religiosity.[29] This pattern holds in samples drawn from different cultural contexts and in meta-analyses of empirical studies on this topic.[30] In this sense, the curvilinear relationship between religiosity and fear of death is a specific instance of the more general curvilinear relationship between fear and religious participation. Likewise, overall health and well-being exhibit a curvilinear relationship with religiosity, particularly when affirmative forms of secularity such as self-identified atheism is taken into account.[31]

The second empirical finding that is relevant for understanding the relationship between religiosity and fear is the curvilinear pattern between religiosity and prejudice.[32] We also found this pattern in CSAF data. For instance, among respondents who were not black, those who attended religious services occasionally were the most likely to stereotype African Americans as criminal. Similarly, nonblack respondents who attended religious services once a month rated African Americans lowest on a "feeling thermometer." Fear and prejudice are intimately linked, and the curvilinear relationship between religiosity and fear provides insight into the curvilinear relationship between religiosity and prejudice.

The third and final curvilinear pattern identified in empirical research that mirrors the relationship between fear and religiosity is the interplay between religion and "paranormal" beliefs and practices. Along with the highest levels of overall fear, the highest levels of paranormalism are found among people who are moderately religious.[33] Individuals who are supernaturalist in orientation while not being tethered to organized religious communities are the most likely to report paranormal beliefs, practices, and experiences.[34] As we will see in our examination of conspiratorial and paranormal subcultures later in the book, there are indeed deep connections among fear, perceived conspiracies, and the paranormal.

So, if we were going to give a hypothetical fearful patient a religious prescription for reducing overall levels of fear, it would be to strongly commit to an inclusive religious community. But if our hypothetical patient could not commit to the extensive and time-consuming demands of very active participation in a tight-knit religious group, then ironically her best bet for reducing fear is actually to become an atheist and stop attending religious services. All in or all out beats in between when it comes to fear and religion.

## Vulnerability and Fear

Aside from the interesting relationship between religion and fear, most of the other important predictors of fear provided strong confirmation for *vulnerability theory*. Much of the psychological and social science research applying vulnerability theory to patterns of fear has focused specifically on fear of crime.[35] This research typically argues that the more vulnerable we are to crime, the more likely we are to fear it. One framing of this research focuses on personal vulnerability or characteristics that might make people less able to either avoid crime or stop a crime from happening. For example, women exhibit more fear of crime than do men. Some argue that this is because women believe themselves less physically able to fight off an attacker, leading to higher levels of fear.[36] At the same time, women are also socialized to have a greater fear of strangers and predators, leading to higher levels of fear.[37] However, this effect is not limited to crime. We found that women are much more fearful than men about *everything*. Whether we are talking about heights or earthquakes, reptiles or burglary, women are more fearful than men. As noted earlier, our Sum of All Fears measure ranges from 0 to 33. The higher the score on this measure, the more fearful a respondent is of all types of things. The average woman in our sample has a score of 14.6; the average man has a score of 11.3. Put another way, women are 29 percent more fearful than men are, on average.

The relationship between age and fear of crime in the existing social science literature is more complicated. Much research has found older people are more afraid of crime.[38] Others have found a more complex relationship, wherein younger and older people are more afraid, with those at middle ages being less afraid.[39] Researchers theorize that older people may be afraid of crime because they are too frail to protect themselves or are more socially isolated and that the young may perceive themselves as too small and weak to stave off crime.[40] We tested for a curvilinear effect for the Sum of All Fears but found no such effect. Instead, the relationship was simpler—young people were more afraid of everything, and fear declines steadily with age. Those who are 65 and older were markedly less afraid (11.7) than were those who were between 18 and 29 at the time of our survey (15.4). The older respondents in our sample were 31 percent less afraid than the youngest respondents.

Age and gender are typically framed as *physical vulnerabilities* in the fear of crime literature. But we must also consider *social vulnerabilities*, including race/ethnicity, income, and education, as well as emphasize the social dimensions of attributes such as gender and age.[41] People with socially vulnerable statuses are assumed to be less able to avoid risky situations or contexts because, on average, they have fewer resources available. For example, someone who has few economic resources may be forced to live in a high-crime neighborhood, thereby increasing his or her fears of criminal victimization. Furthermore, those with fewer social and economic resources may believe themselves less able to cope with the aftermath of negative life events, producing higher levels of fear. For example, someone who has no savings might, logically, be more afraid of an economic downturn or losing his or her job. An abundance of research has found that racial minorities and those with lower levels of income and education "report [a] higher level of fear of crime than their counterparts who are white, affluent, and well educated."[42] When we look at fear of crime, we also find strong support for the social vulnerability hypothesis. However, we find that the fear felt by those who are more socially vulnerable extends far beyond crime. Income, education, employment, and race were also significantly associated with fears of all types. For example, those who earn less than $30,000 a year are

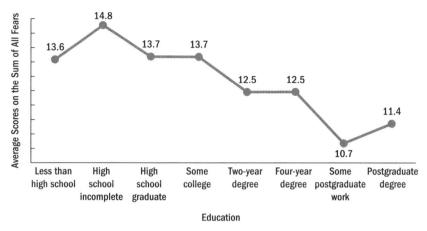

Figure 1.4. Education and Average Scores on the Sum of All Fears (2017).

38 percent more afraid of everything, from murder to zombies, than are those who earn more than $150,000 a year (scoring 15.4 and 11.2 on the Sum of All Fears, respectively). Those who were not currently employed full-time were also significantly more afraid (11 percent) than employed respondents were.

Perhaps becoming more educated leads to a greater capacity for accurately assessing risk and being more skeptical of fear-mongering. Or, perhaps, the tendency of higher education to be associated with better and more stable employment simply provides the economic resources necessary to cope with crises. What is clear is the pronounced relationship between education and fear. The highest levels of fears are among those who started but did not finish high school, while people who have done some postgraduate work have the lowest levels of fear (see Figure 1.4).

The finding of those researching fear of crime that racial minorities are more afraid also extends across the fear spectrum. In fact, racial and ethnic minorities are more afraid of everything. The average white respondent had a score of 12 on the Sum of All Fears, which was significantly lower than African Americans (15.6), Hispanics (14.9), and those of other racial/ethnic groups (14.1). These differences likely reflect institutional racism in the United States, such as differential access to housing, education, and work, and in corresponding differential exposure to poverty, crime, violence, and incarceration. Whites literally and figuratively have less to fear than minorities in twenty-first-century America.

## Fighting Fear

To combat fear, we must first understand who is afraid of what and why. As we have seen in this chapter, when it comes to politics, fears divide us. When a particular fear becomes heavily politicized, there is a concomitant rise in fear among liberals and conservatives. Politicians who have sought to divide us along lines of fear have succeeded. When we set politics aside, however, there is a much more general conclusion. Fear preys on the vulnerable. Those who feel more physically vulnerable and therefore less able to defend themselves are very fearful. Those who feel more socially vulnerable, either because they have minority status or because they lack the material and social capital necessary to either avoid or reckon with disaster, are far more fearful than privileged groups and classes.

Increased levels of fear among people who are physically and socially vulnerable have pernicious consequences. Not only are vulnerable individuals more likely to be exposed to and experience structural forms of violence and inequality; the fear resulting from this differential exposure also levies an additional penalty on personal well-being. Fear is yet another form of risk and punishment disproportionately doled out to the least of these.

2

# Things Are Not What They Seem

Know what is in front of your face, and what is hidden from
you will be disclosed to you.
—*Gospel of Thomas*[1]

## We Never Went to the Moon

The claim that the National Aeronautics and Space Administration
(NASA) faked the Apollo moon landings is a perennial favorite in conspiracy circles.[2] The technology of the 1960s was simply not sufficient
to reach the moon and protect the astronauts from radiation, the argument goes. Once NASA realized that it could not pull off the missions,
it staged a fake moon landing in the desert to avoid embarrassing the
United States.

Ken Johnston has no patience for such claims.

The jovial 75-year-old was speaking to an eager crowd of about 100 at
a conference in Indian Wells, California, we attended. Most of Johnston's
talk focused on his life in the aeronautics industry and what it was like to
work for NASA contractors throughout the space race and moon landings.[3] At the end of his talk, Johnston opened the floor to questions from
the audience and immediately faced skepticism about the moon landings. First up was a woman who asked Johnston how astronauts could
have traveled through the Van Allen belt on their way to the moon without being killed by radiation, a common question of Apollo conspiracy
theorists.[4] Johnston responded that astronauts pass so quickly through
the belt that the amount of radiation they experience is "no more than
standing in front of a microwave." Seemingly irritated by the question,
he stated, "Apollo moon landing deniers make me so mad."

The deniers were undeterred. After a few questions on different topics, an older man came to the microphone and wondered how we "could

be sure" that the photos of the moon provided by NASA are, in fact, originals and not fakes created as part of a cover-up. Johnston countered that "satellites and telescopes have taken pictures of the Apollo landing sites." Once again annoyed by this line of questioning, he tersely stated, "We went to the moon. No doubt about it." After a few more questions in this vein, Johnston ran out of patience. He explained that moon rocks had been sent to scientists all over the globe. If the rocks were fakes, he continued, surely these scientists would be able to tell the difference between a moon rock and an Earth rock and would have exposed the conspiracy. In his final word on the matter, Johnston quieted the Apollo deniers by comparing them to others making dubious claims: "If you are someone who doesn't believe we landed on the moon then you should be careful—you might fall off the edge of our flat earth." He smiled, to generous laughter from the audience.

## Conspiratorial Gnosticism

The style of thinking espoused by the moon landing conspiracists in Johnston's audience is nothing new. Far from it.

Consider a historical example. In Christianity's early history, the burgeoning religion faced the challenge of Gnosticism. There was never a single tradition of Gnosticism. Rather, it consisted of a style of thought and multiple traditions that shared certain commonalities considered heretical by Christian leaders and, therefore, posed a threat to the emergent religion.[5] Gnostics tended to share with Christianity the belief in a singular creator and an evil counterpart, referred to by many names, including the Demiurge. But from there, the differences were pronounced. The God of Gnostics was unknowable, and the material universe was the creation of the Demiurge. For our purposes, the defining characteristic of Gnosticism was its focus on the discovery of *hidden* knowledge and hidden "Truth."[6] The more general term, *gnosis*, refers to "knowledge of the divine mysteries reserved for an élite."[7] Indeed, for Gnostics, the discovery of secret knowledge was more important than faith and held the ultimate key to spiritual enlightenment.

Contemporary conspiracy theories operate as a form of modern Gnosticism. There is much that is "religious" in character about conspiracy theories, including their reliance on empirically unverifiable claims.

Furthermore, both religions and conspiracies outline master, meta-narratives that suggest an interconnectedness between disparate events and the coordination of these events by an outside power.[8] Some conspiracy theories are even explicitly religious in character, such as claims that world events are manipulated by an "Antichrist" or that Satanists are secretly abusing children in macabre ceremonies.[9] A notable difference, however, is the diffuse character of communities articulating conspiracy narratives in contrast to the organized, institutionalized nature of most established religions, where purported truths are provided by designated authorities (and their holy books) and disseminated systematically via religious services. Conspiracy theories are often shared via mediated communication, such as websites, blogs, books, and videos, although they can also be disseminated in face-to-face communities via conferences and other group gatherings.

The Truth of conspiracy theories runs counter to conventional interpretations of history. The designation of a set of ideas as a "conspiracy theory" necessarily marks that belief system as deviant, unconventional, and subcultural.[10] Something effectively given this label is *stigmatized knowledge*. When conspiracy theories are held by powerful groups, they are effectively moral panics rather than "conspiracy theories." Conspiracy theories and moral panics share many common social processes, including stereotyping, media magnification of fantastical stories, selective observation, scapegoating, and apocalyptic rhetoric.[11] For instance, prior to the 1960s, beliefs that would today be classed as conspiracy theories were often held by people in power and used to suppress a long list of supposed subversives, from Satanists to Catholics and slaves to communists.[12] Since then, particularly in the aftermath of the assassination of John F. Kennedy, the term *conspiracy theory* has been used by scholars to label accounts of historical events that present an alternative interpretation of episodes, processes, and knowledge compared to what is popularly advanced by mainstream social institutions, such as the scientific community or government. These alternative understandings of how the world and social systems operate are quite popular in contemporary, as well as historical America.[13]

A key distinction between moral panics and conspiracy theories lies with the social power of the claimants. Moral panics *consolidate* power through the mutually reciprocal processes of punishment and in-group solidarity. Conspiracy theories are held by those without power and provide narrative frameworks for perceived freedom and agentic identity through defiant *resistance* to power.[14]

There are four principles of what we term *conspiratorial Gnosticism.* First, conspiracy theories often contain a "kernel of truth." Although globalist conspiracies may overstate the power or malevolence of the world's financial and political elite, it is nonetheless indisputably true that the world is disproportionately influenced by the wealthiest individuals. Likewise, although the terrorist attacks of 9/11 were not a "false flag" operation perpetuated by government insiders, it is nonetheless indisputably true that the U.S. government misled the public about the causes of 9/11, particularly in rhetoric justifying the invasion of Iraq and many other post-9/11 military and criminal justice policies.[15] Thus, conspiracy theories often begin with fundamental truths before pushing beyond such truths and into the realm of speculation and over-perceived interconnections. In this sense, for those wishing to combat conspiracy theories, remembering that they must still take note of the legitimate underlying grievances rather than discounting *all* criticism directed toward conventional interpretations of reality is important. Of course, these truths are routinely denied, as are many other truths pertaining to injustice in the world. This makes accepting the foundational edict of conspiracy theories—"things are not what they seem"—not only plausible but inherently appealing as well.

Second, the acceptance of the premise that things are not what they seem provides an avenue for seeing the world anew. Like religious experiences and divine revelations, specific conspiratorial worldviews confer on believers "new eyes" with which to interpret seemingly normal events as evidence of pernicious, shadowy forces orchestrating the puppetry dancing on Plato's proverbial cave wall. Perceiving oneself as awakened to the True reality that eludes those who accept the world at face value, conspiracies facilitate the feeling of holding an exclusive Truth, one of the primary appeals to believers.[16]

Third, with this new Truth in place and the assistance of "spirit guides" of conspiracy—in the form of television personalities, radio hosts, book authors, bloggers, and amateur documentarians—conspiracy theories spin larger webs of proposed and speculated interconnections. In effect, conspiracies over-posit the connectedness of the social world. The plausibility of such speculation rests on the tendency of human minds to overestimate causal connections between disparate events.[17] Through this process, purportedly hidden causes and connections are brought into view. The benefit of seeing such connections is the banishment of ambiguity. Where uncertainty previously reigned, a clear explanation now resides. Explanatory completeness and, with it, a solidified sense of personal and social identity are also primary benefits of conspiracy theories for believers.[18] As cultural historian Michael Butter noted in his analysis of conspiracy theories throughout American history, "Conspiracy theories produce exceptionally strong notions of Self, the people, and Other, the conspirators because they imagine the Other not only as different and hostile but as already plotting the Self's destruction or enslavement."[19]

Finally, believers must decide what to do with the radical, stigmatizing knowledge they now accept and see in the world.[20] Fighting the perceived forces of injustice, spreading the word about the secret Truth of gnosis, and preparing for future battles against perceived enemies are among the most common responses to seeing conspiracies in the world—that and, of course, consuming more media about alleged conspiracies. Living a conspiracy leads to highly motivated forms of reasoning and a tendency to see additional connections through over-inference and selective observation. Furthermore, conspiracy theories contain a "monologic" that is "self-sealing." A distilled notion of this logic is the edict that the absence of evidence is evidence of the power of the conspirators.[21] There is no escape from such reasoning.

From our own and others' studies of different conspiracy subcultures, we can identify the fundamental building blocks of conspiracist ideologies. Distilled to its essence, the archetypal conspiracy narrative is as follows:

> What you think you know and have been told about the world is an illusion. This is the Great Truth. Everywhere, talking heads and tweeting twits are spinning lies, denying Truth, and trying to advance their own evil agenda. But once you know the Truth, deceptions hiding in plain sight are revealed. Wake up! Fight back!! Otherwise, the unthinkable *will* happen, and everything you know and love will be destroyed. The Awakened are our only hope.

This is the basic narrative template on which conspiracy theories weave endlessly creative permutations. Notably, such a narrative also conforms to some elements of religious myths that detail what comparative religions scholar Joseph Campbell called the "hero's journey."[22]

The power of conspiracy narratives is clear. Conspiracy theories provide believers a compelling narrative of agentic dignity in the face of injustice and suffering. By dividing the world into binary categories of good and evil and then naming folk devils, revealing their plan, and unmasking their concealment, believers become noble heroes standing strong in the face of tyranny.[23] By fighting the good fight and taking action, believers make meaning both in their lives and in the social realities and traumas they see around them.[24] In short, "conspiracy thinking gives hope, unity, and purpose in a world that often seems beyond the reach of the powerless."[25] The popularity of conspiracy theories is at least partially due to the fact that they are effective cultural schemas for *making sense of the world and providing an identity narrative of dignity and moral action.*

Scholars have attempted to situate the current popularity of such views within the context of technologically advanced societies that have ready access to an overwhelming amount of information on any given topic—some endorsed by established social institutions and some formulated by those outside of conventional and dominant knowledge channels.[26] This position places individuals in a situation where they must discern for themselves which knowledge is accurate and reliable. As people navigate the world of information overload and global capitalism, many turn to conspiratorial frameworks to make sense of dramatic political actors and events, as well as their own experiences. For some, conspiratorial beliefs are relatively peripheral and held in conjunction with other nonstigmatized forms of knowledge. For others, conspiratorial outlooks become all-encompassing belief systems, the primary lenses through which both self and society are refracted.

The totalizing power of conspiracy was quite evident at the 2018 Contact in the Desert conference featuring Ken Johnston.

Indeed, we omitted an important part of the story of Johnston's strident rejection of claims that the Apollo moon landings were a hoax. Johnston's problem with Apollo deniers is not actually about denying conspiracies about the moon. Instead, his concern is about *which* moon conspiracy is true. It seems that NASA—which Johnston said stands for "Never A Straight Answer"—*did* make it to the moon. And when the astronauts did land, they found evidence of an extraterrestrial presence there. He showed a picture of an astronaut standing on the moon's surface with a blob reflected in his visor. The blob, he claimed, is the "reflection of a spacecraft" that was observing the astronauts. In another picture of an astronaut holding a bag of rocks, a blurry series of dots and lines are visible in the far distant sky. This is an alien base, he told an enraptured audience, and it "looks just like" the alien base used by the villain in the James Bond movie *Moonraker*. The similarity is no accident, he continued. Hollywood knows more than it is telling us about the alien presence and, for reasons unclear to us, chose to model the *Moonraker* base after the alien facility.[27] The variety of pictures of hazy objects and blobs on the moon and in its orbit displayed by Johnston portrayed the moon as a vibrant hub of alien activity.

Such astounding revelations do not come without risk. The evil henchmen at NASA may one day come for Johnston, he warned. "When you put out information they [NASA] want to shut you up." He claimed that many of those who have tried to reveal the alien presence on the moon have died in suspicious auto accidents or suddenly developed "strange diseases." Hopefully Johnston will avoid such a fate so he can continue to chastise Apollo deniers and spread the truth about the *real* NASA conspiracy.

That someone could ridicule one conspiracy theory and call into question the sanity of its claimants, only to espouse another, more fantastical theory might seem odd. But our study and observations of conspiracy subcultures suggest that it is becoming less an issue of whether Americans believe in conspiracies, and more a matter of which ones.

## Conspiracy Nation

Drawing on studies of conspiracy theories in political science, psychology, sociology, and religious studies, we asked about belief in a wide range of conspiracies on the Chapman University Survey of American Fears. A battery of questions asked for respondents' levels of agreement with whether "the government is concealing what it knows about . . ." Included in the list were alien encounters, the 9/11 terrorist attacks,

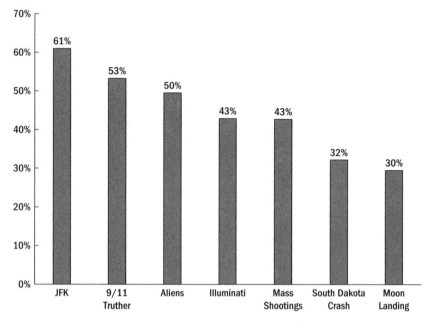

Figure 2.1. Americans' Belief in Conspiracy Theories (2018): "The government is concealing what it knows about. . . ."

the JFK assassination, the South Dakota crash, the moon landing, the Illuminati/New World Order, and mass shootings such as those in Las Vegas and Sandy Hook. If you have not heard about the South Dakota crash, you are not alone. We made it up and inserted it into the list of possible conspiracies to gauge respondents' willingness to believe in a conspiracy that does not actually exist.[28] (Or does it?)

Figure 2.1 shows the percentage of Americans who believe the government is hiding information about specific items and events. As evidence of the popularity of conspiracy theories, more than half of respondents expressed belief in *four or more of the conspiracies presented*.[29] The belief that the government is concealing information about the JFK assassination (61 percent) was the most popular. Following close behind was the belief that the government is concealing information about the 9/11 terrorist attacks (53 percent). Half of Americans believe the government knows something about aliens. Forty-three percent of Americans believe in a New World Order/Illuminati conspiracy and that the government is concealing information about mass shootings such as Sandy Hook. Almost a third (30 percent) would agree with the audience at Contact in the Desert: something fishy happened during the moon landing. We were quite surprised to find that one-third of respondents agreed that the government is concealing information about the "South Dakota crash," suggesting a high susceptibility to conspiratorial thinking in general. In further support of this, only 24 percent of Americans rejected all seven conspiracies.

## A Conspiracy of Our Own Making: The South Dakota Crash

Of greatest interest to us is the possible relationship between fear and a conspiratorial mind-set. To the extent that fear is a reaction to uncertainty often unmoored from an actual threat, conspiratorial thinking may follow high levels of fear. To better understand Americans' proclivities toward conspiracy, we analyzed the patterns of responses to the question about the South Dakota crash. What personal characteristics made respondents more likely to report that the government is concealing what it knows about the conspiracy we made up? We assessed the statistical relationships between believing in a South Dakota crash conspiracy and demographic factors, political views, and a host of other factors, the most important of which, for the current purposes, was fear.[30] To examine the extent to which fear is related to believing in conspiracy theories, we again added all nonpartisan fears together into the Sum of All Fears. As before, higher scores on this measure mean greater fear of all types of things, from earthquakes to clowns to government corruption.

In terms of demographics, Americans with high levels of education and income were significantly less likely to believe in the South Dakota crash conspiracy compared to those with lower socioeconomic status. Women, African Americans, southerners, and those who take the Bible literally were more likely to believe in our faux conspiracy. Demonstrating a natural affinity between fear and conspiracy theories, the Sum of All Fears was quite strongly related to belief in a fake conspiracy.[31] Less than one-fourth of those who had below-average levels of fear (22 percent) believed in our South Dakota crash conspiracy. People who were about average in their levels of fear were much more likely to believe in the South Dakota crash; 38 percent of them did.[32] Those with higher levels of fear exhibit exorbitantly higher levels of belief in the nefarious events in South Dakota. Fully 62 percent of those with above-average levels of fear believe in this conspiracy.[33] Once someone truly reaches a pronounced level of fear (far above average), belief in conspiracies is quite strong. Fully 77 percent of respondents who had very high levels of fear believed in the government cover-up of the South Dakota crash.[34]

The tight connection between fear and conspiratorial thinking is clear. Given that conspiracy theories generally tend to "overread" reality, finding patterns where none exist, we can begin to understand this relationship better. Fear is produced by the brain's threat-detection systems, and hence, fearful people are vigilantly on the lookout for both patterns and perceived danger, both notable hallmarks of conspiracy theories. When in a state of heightened awareness, the brain strives to impose order on ambiguity and chaos.[35] In this sense, conspiratorial thinking is an ideological response to fear and perceived threat.

## The Conspiratorial Mind

Has the Catholic Church covered up evidence that Jesus survived the crucifixion and fathered a child? Is the medical community hiding the danger of vaccines? Does a race of reptilian aliens live under Denver International Airport, or under the city of Los Angeles, or both? What does the government know about contrails?

One could be forgiven for becoming overwhelmed by the dizzying variety of conspiracy theories that exist in the public consciousness, as they vary so widely in scope, content, and claims. Yet all conspiracies share one grand similarity. Whether they involve our past, present, or future; the government or aliens; our environment; our bodies or our minds, all conspiracies assume the existence of extremely powerful "others" who are usually portrayed as evil. These others, whose identity varies by conspiracy, use their resources to hide the Truth from the rest of us. And the power available to these others must be immense. For the government to have successfully covered up the assassination of JFK by—well, pick your conspiracy here—for more than half a century would require the existence of a massive conspiracy enacted by persistent, shadowy forces within. To hide a race of reptilian people under one of the world's busiest airports would require supernatural powers of diversion.

The focus that conspiracy theories have on mysterious, evil others with functionally, if not literally, supernatural powers suggests that an orientation toward conspiracy thinking may be related to other key factors in addition to (but also related to) fear. First, we should expect that someone who believes in the devil may be more likely to accept conspiracy theories, given that binary thinking is a hallmark of both religion and conspiracism. Second, belief in paranormal subjects, such as aliens, ghosts, and Bigfoot, should be related to conspiracy-oriented thinking. Belief in the paranormal indicates a willingness to embrace alternative sources of information other than those officially sanctioned by societal institutions, such as academic science or the federal government. When individuals embrace stigmatized knowledge, they also become more likely to embrace alternative understandings of how the social systems permeating their existence operate. In a very real sense, belief in the paranormal and conspiracy theories both offer something to those who have been alienated and marginalized from conventional society. In general, "conspiracy thinking proves an antidote to powerlessness. It lifts the despair of vulnerability and arms believers with the knowledge to understand and defeat the enemy."[36] Indeed, we found compelling evidence that the conspiratorial mind often involves a complicated mixture of fear, supernatural evil, and paranormalism.

To better understand the patterns and predictors of a conspiratorial mind-set, we first counted the number of conspiracies our respondents believed. Respondents received a 1 if they believe in a particular conspiracy and a 0 if they did not.[37] Our final count for each respondent ranged from 0 to 7. A respondent who received a score of 2 may have expressed belief in a JFK conspiracy and a cover-up about aliens but disbelieved other conspiracies. Another respondent with a score of 2 may have been, instead, convinced by 9/11 truther claims and stories about a hoaxed moon landing. There was considerable variation in conspiracy belief, with only about 24 percent of Americans believing in none of them and about 16 percent *believing in all seven.* Most respondents fell somewhere in between. We created a model to predict how many conspiracies people believed in by using their demographic characteristics, political identity, religious views, levels of fear, paranormalism, and belief in Satan.

Our analysis showed that several demographic characteristics were predictive of conspiracy beliefs. Higher education has the power to curb the acceptance of conspiracy narratives, with higher levels of education and income being associated with less conspiracy beliefs. As previous research has also found, age is associated with conspiracies, with younger people being more likely to believe.[38] Although we are unable to say so definitively without trend data over a long period, these age effects likely reflect generational shifts rather than changes over the life course. In other words, younger generations have now, and we expect they will maintain, higher levels of belief in conspiracism throughout their lives than do older generations. African Americans also showed a significantly higher level of belief in conspiracies than whites, Hispanics, or those of other racial groups. On average, African Americans in our sample believed in four conspiracy theories, compared to three for non–African Americans.

### Fear and Conspiracy

Fear was not just predictive of our "imaginary" calamity of the South Dakota crash. Rather, it is quite clear that there is a tight, intimate connection between being fearful and being conspiracy-oriented. The data we have available do not allow us to test for the direction of this effect. In other words, we cannot say if being a fearful person makes you more likely to accept conspiracies, or if believing that the moon landing was a hoax or that 9/11 was an inside job is what makes you afraid. The two undoubtedly work together, with fear feeding the tendency to believe in unseen and powerful forces and conspiratorial beliefs exacerbating fear.

Stated plainly, if you are afraid of a lot of things, you will be more likely to accept conspiracy theories. As noted earlier, we categorized people by their overall levels of fear. Someone who is very high on the Sum of All Fears exhibits high levels of fear about everything, from clowns to volcanoes. Someone very low on this measure is afraid of very few things. People below average in their level of fear believe in two conspiracies on average. Once you have reached mid-levels of fear (at the average or slightly above), you will tend to believe in four conspiracies. Those unfortunate souls who exhibited the highest levels of fear in our study believed in an average of five of the seven conspiracies.[39]

## Satan's Power

Although we examined the most common measures of religion, such as affiliation (what religious group a person belongs to), how often someone attends religious services, and whether the respondent believes that the Bible is the literal word of God, the effects of these standard measures of religion were minimal. Going to church more or less often will not protect you from believing or cause you to believe in conspiracies. Thinking that the Bible was written by God himself is related to marginally higher levels of conspiratorial belief than thinking the Bible is just a book of stories, but the effect is relatively small. Protestants are significantly less likely to believe in conspiracies than those of other religious traditions, but being Catholic, Jewish, nonreligious, or something else has no effect one way or the other.

In addition to these standard religion metrics, we also asked respondents for their level of agreement with the statement "Satan causes most evil in the world." Belief in a supernatural force for evil was one of the strongest predictors in our analyses.[40] Those who either agreed or strongly agreed that Satan causes most evil believed in four conspiracy theories, on average. People who disagreed with this statement believed in three conspiracy theories, while those who entirely rejected the notion of Satan sowing evil in the world (strongly disagreeing) believed in two conspiracy theories, on average. Furthermore, we examined the relationship between *fear* of religious evil and belief in conspiracism. Interestingly, this aspect accounts for the general relationship between belief in religious evil and conspiracism. Once again, and in yet another way, fear is central to understanding conspiracism.

## Media Consumption

Patterns of media consumption were also significantly related to levels of conspiracism. Americans who regularly read national newspapers were less likely to accept conspiracy theories. Slow news is good news, at least for rational thinking. In contrast, people who regularly watch daytime talk shows and frequently get their news from social media believe in significantly more conspiracies. People who said they get their news from social media every day believed in an average of 4.3 out of the 7 conspiracies! Similarly, the frequency of smartphone use was also significantly related to higher levels of conspiracism. People who reported using their cell phones five or more hours per day also believed in an average of 4.5 out of the 7 conspiracies. Respondents who did both—used their cell phones more than five hours each day and got news from social media every day—believed in nearly five out of the seven conspiracies, *on average*. Although we hate to sound like grumpy Luddites griping about "kids these days," put your damn phone down and log off Facebook! It is bad for your brain; democracy, too.

*Paranormalism*

Belief in the paranormal—that which is explicitly rejected by both organized science and mainstream religion—is intimately tied to belief in conspiracy theory.[41] We determined how strongly respondents believed in the paranormal by asking them questions about aliens (ancient and modern), psychics, hauntings, Bigfoot, Atlantis, and telekinesis. For example, the Bigfoot question asked respondents for their level of agreement with the statement "Bigfoot is a real creature," while the haunting question asked if they agree that "places can be haunted by spirits."[42] We added responses to these seven questions together.[43] Someone who scored a zero did not believe in any of these paranormal phenomena. Someone who scored 21 demonstrated a strong belief in all seven. As previous research has found, Americans exhibit a high level of paranormal belief.[44] Only 10 percent of Americans were entirely skeptical of all the paranormal claims we presented to them. The average respondent scored about 8, meaning they have a moderate level of paranormal belief, believing very strongly in a few items or at least moderately believing in several.

Paranormal beliefs are strongly related to conspiracism and had, by far, the strongest effect in our analyses. Figure 2.2 shows the tight relationship between paranormal beliefs and conspiracy beliefs. Those who greatly reject the paranormal (very low in the chart in Figure 2.2) also tend to reject conspiracy-oriented thinking, believing in only one conspiracy on average. For those dabbling with the paranormal, the number of conspiracies believed rises to two. Those who expressed moderate interest and belief in the paranormal are also quite interested

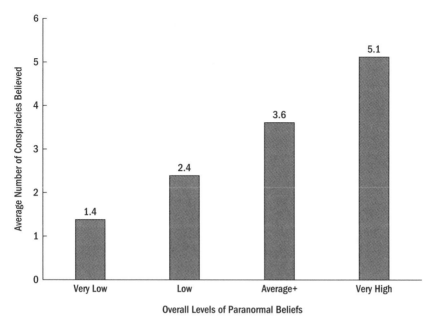

Figure 2.2. Number of Conspiracies Believed by Paranormalism (2018).

in conspiracies, believing in, on average, about four. Those at the highest levels of paranormalism could also be properly categorized as conspiracists, believing in, on average, five of the seven conspiracies.

So, if you know someone who believes in ghosts or Bigfoot, there's a high likelihood that he or she also lends some credence to one conspiracy or another. But one paranormal subculture in particular stands apart in its connection to conspiracism. In the unidentified flying object (UFO) subculture, conspiracism and paranormalism are so deeply and fundamentally intertwined that they are scarcely distinguishable.

Conspiracy-oriented thinking within the UFO community reaches back to its earliest days. Most histories of the modern UFO movement trace its origins to Kenneth Arnold's sighting of strange objects near Mount Rainier in Washington State on June 24, 1947.[45] In the wake of Arnold's encounter, a rash of UFO sightings and events led to the formation of many UFO research organizations and clubs. Albert K. Bender founded one such club, the International Flying Saucer Bureau, just a few years after Arnold's sighting, in 1952, but shut it down just one year later. Bender ultimately revealed to a friend and publisher of UFO books, Gray Barker, that he had been intimidated into closing his organization by a visit from three mysterious "men in black." Barker reported the claim in his 1956 book, *They Knew Too Much about Flying Saucers*.[46] For nearly half a century before they became the stars of a blockbuster film series, UFO witnesses told stories of visits from the sinister men in black (MIB) who threatened them into silence. The MIB are but a small facet of extensive UFO-based conspiracy lore that could easily fill this volume. Conspiracists also claim that the U.S. government covered up a 1947 UFO crash at Roswell, New Mexico, have kept the alien origins of mysterious cattle mutilations occurring across the United States from the public, maintained a fleet of reverse-engineered flying saucers (and perhaps even live extraterrestrials) at Area 51 outside of Las Vegas, and signed a treaty with alien beings permitting them to abduct a select number of humans. And this is barely a start. We'll spare you the rest of the details.[47]

Although there has always been an undercurrent of conspiracy in UFO lore, these conspiracies have generally focused on the claim that the U.S. government was hiding or suppressing evidence. But in more recent years, UFO conspiracies have incorporated claims not typically associated with extraterrestrials, such as the JFK assassination and 9/11, into a bewildering alternate (dimension) history of the world. No one better exemplifies this trend than best-selling author David Wilcock.

## "Science Is Now Behind Us!"

As the *Star Trek Voyager* theme blasted from speakers, hundreds filled the largest amphitheater at the resort in Indian Wells, California, hosting the 2018 Contact in the Desert conference.[48] The enthusiastic audience packed the room to hear David Wilcock's talk, titled "Revealing the Five Alliance Groups." Wilcock is "a channeller, UFO enthusiast and jazz-rock drummer from California," who believes he is the reincarnation of somnambulant soothsayer Edgar Cayce. He couches his message of spiritual enlightenment in magical narratives of intergalactic battles between good and evil. These stories led him to become "one of the most prominent figures in millennial conspiracist discourse in the late-2000s and 2010s."[49]

Wilcock preaches a form of UFO-themed enlightenment that closely conforms to our archetype of conspiratorial Gnosticism. His stories also draw on the narratives of UFO contactees who started quasi-religious movements, such as George Adamski, as well as the Theosophical movement of Helena Blavatsky.[50] Wilcock's tales blend science fiction and religious ideas, but like all conspiracy theories, the goal is to deliver "special knowledge—this gnosis—that transforms the individual from being one of the passive, sleeping 'sheeple' into an active, autonomous agent of change."[51] Having previously heard stories about a council of benevolent aliens known as the "Alliance," we expected to hear tales of encounters with friendly extraterrestrials. But on appearing onstage to thunderous applause, Wilcock immediately and breathlessly began outlining a labyrinthian alternative history of the world, refracted through a lens of extraterrestrial visitation. It seems that aliens have been interacting with the Earth throughout time.

For Wilcock, history is best understood as a covert war between the Alliance and select earthling associates who are trying to reveal the Truth about alien visitation versus an evil conspiracy consisting of malicious aliens and *their* earthly co-conspirators.[52] Fifty thousand years ago, an alien race called the Dracos attacked peaceful aliens that were living on our moon. Those aliens fled to Earth and interbred with humans: "We are all descendants of ETs [extraterrestrials]—there are no purebred humans," Wilcock told the enraptured audience. The alien refugees have been influencing our cultures ever since. They built the pyramids and established a series of portals that they could use to travel between the Earth and other planetary systems. One of these alien portals resides in the Vatican. But fearing the religious repercussions of admitting to an alien presence, Catholic leaders have hidden this portal, as well as a large collection of books written by ancient aliens that are stored in the Vatican library.

At a breakneck pace, Wilcock sped through history, from the pyramids to World War II. He reported that John Dee, an astrologer and advisor to Queen Elizabeth I, learned how to "summon negative entities, which we call aliens." The perennial conspiracy theory chestnut of the Illuminati was formed expressly to work with evil alien beings. The American Revolution was not, in fact, a reaction to oppressive taxation but a revolt against the Illuminati. Wilcock then fast-forwarded to the

Civil War, at which time Abraham Lincoln visited a cave on the banks of the Ohio River containing the levitating bodies of giant alien beings. He was later assassinated by the Illuminati when he came too close to revealing the Truth.

The alien conspiracy kicked into high gear by World War II. In 1939, the Nazis met with a contingent of Dracos in the Himalayas and started working with them. The Dracos shared alien technology with the Nazis, who "were traveling to the moon and other planets by the 1940s." Indeed, World War II was itself a "big con." The Illuminati "owned both sides of the war" and engineered mass casualties to reduce the human population. Furthermore, Hitler survived World War II.[53] He lived until the 1960s alongside a large group of Nazis who moved, along with their advanced technology, to South America and Antarctica. The Nazis staged a mass UFO sighting over Washington, D.C., in 1952 and scared a segment of the U.S. government into joining their "shadow government."

Ever since this agreement was made among aliens, Nazis, and certain segments of the U.S. government, all subsequent presidents have been either working for or against the conspiracy. In a rapid-fire series of slides, Wilcock revealed the presidential heroes and villains. Dwight D. Eisenhower (hero) threatened to send an army contingent to attack Area 51 but backed off once the nature of alien encounters was revealed to him. John F. Kennedy (hero) was assassinated because he planned to reveal the Truth about UFOs. The Watergate scandal was engineered by the conspirators to keep Nixon (hero) quiet about aliens. Jimmy Carter (hero) was well known for having an interest in UFOs and claimed his own sighting. George H. W. Bush (villain) set up the Iran hostage situation to drive Carter out of office before he could reveal the Truth. Despite having a villain as vice president, Ronald Reagan was one of the heroes. The comedian Jackie Gleason had been shown alien bodies by Richard Nixon and told his friend Reagan about it. The assassination attempt on Reagan was designed to warn him against revealing anything about aliens to the public. "The next time we won't miss," the conspirators told Reagan. During Reagan's time in office, in 1985, a massive alien spacecraft called the Seeker arrived in our solar system. The Cold War was merely a diversion, as all the money dedicated to an arms race with the Soviets was actually diverted to a joint U.S./Soviet "secret space program" that chased away the Seeker.

Gerald Ford escaped being labeled either a hero or a villain, but with regard to the Clintons, their designation was abundantly clear: villains. The Clintons were villains long before entering office, Wilcock offered, to cheers and claps from the audience. They ran an elaborate cocaine business out of Arkansas. The suicide of Deputy White House Counsel Vince Foster, long the subject of conspiracy theories, was actually a murder engineered by Hillary. Foster is one of the heroes of the Alliance, Wilcock said, as he put up a picture of the deceased lawyer to applause. On April 17, 1995, a group of air force officers boarded a plane headed to Washington, D.C. The officers were part of the Alliance group and planned to stage a coup to take down the evil Clintons. Their plane crashed, killing all aboard, the seeming accident once again engineered by Bill and Hillary. The Oklahoma City bombing, which happened only a few days later, was staged as a diversion to draw attention away from the recent plane crash.

The election of George W. Bush (villain) to office did not improve matters. The attacks of 9/11 were an attempt by the shadow, alien-aligned government to destroy those aspects of the government associated with the Alliance. "The exact part of the Pentagon that was hit was the Alliance headquarters," reported Wilcock. And most of the key Alliance documents about aliens were in the World Trade Center, which is why it was also attacked.

Brighter days appear to be ahead with the election of Donald Trump, however. One of the (many) controversial aspects of the Trump presidency is his frequent statements about creating another branch of the military he calls the "Space Force." Wilcock believes that Trump's quest for a Space Force arises from a desire to combat the evil, alien shadow government. "Trump wants to build a base on Mars," he continued. The crowd cheered enthusiastically.

Wilcock's history of the world gathers together almost all major conspiracy narratives into a single super-conspiracy. A complete recounting of his talk would include asides into the POW-MIA conspiracy; the Knights Templar; the true authorship of Shakespeare's works (by Francis Bacon); the leaking of information about aliens through Hollywood movies; mind control; time travel; the Freemasons; the destruction of Atlantis; sightings of the Virgin Mary in Fatima, Portugal; and the Iran–Contra affair. Wilcock's ideology is a window into a world where the mainstream media, scientists, and other conventional sources of information cannot be trusted, and indeed, *nothing* is as it seems.

Wilcock may seem to be on the fringes of American thought or the very far fringes, to some readers. But in recent years, the toxic combination of fear, conspiracy, and paranormalism has reached the highest branches of government, thanks to a certain friend of Donald Trump named Alex Jones.

### There's a War on for Your Mind!

Alex Jones began his career as a cable-access TV host in Austin, Texas. He then moved to radio, followed soon thereafter by the Internet. In addition to his show, Jones has produced or directed more than 30 "documentaries" detailing the conspiracies he sees permeating American society, such as the *Obama Deception* and the *Police State* tetralogy.[54] In a one-year span from April 2017 until April 2018, Jones's InfoWars web page had more than 320 million views globally. The audience's demographics skewed heavily toward older men.[55] Jones's antiestablishment message clearly caught on with a mass public alienated by mainstream politics.

Jones's overall ideology is difficult to elaborate succinctly, but some basic components are worth mentioning. First, paranormalism and demonology sometimes appear in Jones's rants, whether it be the claim that Donald Trump will soon reveal that thousands of alien species are visiting Earth or that Hillary Clinton and Barack Obama are demons who smell like sulfur.[56] Conspiracies of all stripes, however, dominate Jones's content. He points to the JFK assassination as a critical turning point in American history. On his way to visit the assassination site, Jones said,

> We're going back to Eden. Except it's not a wonderful, beautiful place, it's a horrible place where the military-industrial complex murdered our last real President in broad daylight in front of everyone. We're going back to the birthplace of what you could call the conspiracy culture.[57]

Jones was motivated to publicly oppose what he saw as government oppression and tyranny after the disastrous 1993 Branch Davidian stand-off in nearby Waco, Texas, that resulted in the death of 82 members of the religious sect and four agents of the Bureau of Alcohol, Tobacco, and Firearms. Jones argues that many public tragedies, including terrorist attacks and mass shootings, are actually "false flag" attacks staged by the American government to impose a tyrannical rule on U.S. citizens. Jones has been sued for defamation by the parents of children murdered in the Sandy Hook school shooting. These parents of slain elementary schoolchildren became targets of harassment after Jones repeatedly promoted the idea that the shooting was staged.[58]

In addition to arguing that Barack Obama is a puppet of the New World Order, Jones and his platforms have also promoted "birther" conspiracies about Obama.[59] Jerome Corsi, who holds a doctorate in political science from Harvard, served as the InfoWars Bureau chief in Washington, D.C, in 2017 and 2018. In addition to numerous right-wing books about topics such as the JFK assassination and the dangers of the "deep state," Corsi also authored *Where's the Birth Certificate?: The Case that Barack Obama Is not Eligible to Be President*. After the 2017 mass shooting in Las Vegas, Jones called the event "as phony as a three dollar bill or Obama's birth certificate."[60]

Jones is also known for his role in amplifying the conspiracy that came to be known as "Pizzagate," which alleged that Hillary Clinton and other "top Democratic officials were involved with a satanic child pornography ring centered around Comet Ping Pong, a pizza restaurant in Washington, D.C."[61] Jones did not start the rumors, which began in anonymous online forums such as 4chan and Reddit, but he did promote the (cyber-)urban legends once they grew in online visibility. Believers began threatening the pizza restaurant and its employees and even spread the idea to other pizza locations around the United States.[62] Ultimately, a Pizzagate believer named Edgar Welch traveled from North Carolina to Comet Ping Pong armed with an AR-15 rifle, which he fired in the restaurant, in an attempt to investigate the matter and save any children in peril. Welch said that he heard about the rumors by word of mouth, but tellingly reported that after he recently had Internet installed at his house he was "really able to look into it."[63]

Watching Jones sermonize about the pernicious New World Order left us with some distinct impressions about the thematic content of his message. First, it is essentially a form of secular apocalypticism, and Jones a hellfire and brimstone preacher, complete with the hallmark histrionic delivery of such sectarian showmen. Second, and consistent with the framework of conspiratorial Gnosticism, Jones attempts to debunk official narratives about world events to lead his audience toward seeing the Truth (as he understands it). Finally, there is an inescapable sense of Jones's diatribes as melodramatic, masculinist hero fantasies in which Jones and his followers valiantly resist the forces of pure evil by forming resistance identities that defy and expose the New World Order.

For believers, resistance imbues the mundanities of everyday life with meaningful action on the side of righteousness. Seth Jackson, a fervent believer in Jones, said when interviewed for the documentary *New World Order* about Jones and his followers, "It's woke[n] me up, and it's changed my life. It's made me wanna stand for something, and it's made me wanna fight for my people. It's made me wanna wake other people up to understand what is going on."[64] Later in the film, Jackson aptly encapsulates the fundamental features of conspiratorial Gnosticism as he stands with Jones and others at the National September 11 Memorial & Museum at ground zero in Manhattan on September 11, protesting the official narrative about the terrorist attacks:

> We're surrounded by the enemy, and the people see that, you know? We *will* bring the darkness into the light. We will. Some people here might not know what they're doing, but they'll figure it out too. They'll figure out why they're here, eventually. That's our job. People think this is a joke. It's not a joke, and we're not kidding [crying]. We're for real. We're not just out here to be conspiracy theorists, to protest, to be anarchists. We want Truth. We want a good life. It's so real, and people don't get it. They think it's a joke. They think we're full of shit. They have no clue how real we are. I don't know what else to say. We're defeating the enemy though, every day.[65]

Summarizing all aspects of Jones's worldview is nearly impossible, but it might be best described as far-right libertarian with recurring fever dreams about globalists and a coming "New World Order" system of tyrannical governance that must be opposed by masculinist heroes. Despite criticism of Jones's more extreme views and numerous lawsuits, he maintains a loyal following, particularly in cyberspace. Although he has since been suspended from the platform, Jones's channel on YouTube had more than 2 million subscribers. His organization prolifically publishes multimedia content while also promoting Jones's own line of dietary supplements—to counter the globalists' efforts to lower people's hormone levels, especially testosterone. He infamously railed against such efforts in October 2015, screaming, "What do you think tap water is? It's a gay bomb, baby. . . . I don't like 'em puttin' chemicals in the water that turn the friggin' frogs gay! Do you understand that?! I'm sick of this crap! [pounding on desk] I'm sick of being social engineered! It's not funny!"[66]

## From the Fringes to the White House

No one was laughing two months later in December 2015, when then-candidate Donald Trump, who had recently emerged as the front runner of a very crowded Republican presidential primary field, appeared on Jones's show for a half-hour interview. Appealing to a nontraditional but potentially very sympathetic audience, Trump visited Jones's show on InfoWars, ostensibly to promote his book *Crippled America*. In introducing Trump, Jones noted how much he shared in common with his guest of honor:

> Obviously he is, a maverick. He's an original. He tells it like it is. Doesn't read off a teleprompter. Neither do I. He's self-made. This whole media operation that reaches 20 million people a week worldwide, conservatively; self-made. That's why I'm so excited he joins us from Trump Tower in New York City. He is the leading 2016 presidential contender.

The two men primarily discussed matters of Islamophobia and xenophobia, with Jones supporting Trump's views of foreign policy ideas in the Middle East and portraying Trump as prophetically predicting the disaster of the Iraq War. Jones later said, "Well Donald Trump let me say this, my audience, I'd say ninety percent support you. And you definitely have shown your knowledge of geopolitical systems." Trump returned the flattery, closing the interview by telling Jones, "I just want to finish by saying your reputation is amazing. I will not let you down. You will be very, very impressed, I hope, and I think we'll be speaking a lot."[67] InfoWars' YouTube channel drew 83 million views in November

2016. After the election, Trump personally called to thank Jones for his support. For his part, Jones has said, "I know Trump watches and sees the clips and things."[68] Throughout his presidency, Trump has continued calling to speak with Jones but in private, rather than on the air.[69] In his stead, Trump campaign operative Roger Stone became a regular contributor for InfoWars.

Ironically, having the ear of the president places Jones in a precarious position. Given that he has spent his career on and built his image around opposing government power, he must now walk a very fine line of being critical of mainstream institutions while supporting the most powerful man in the world. Regardless, Jones will not be changing his views about the New World Order. He is far too invested in and dependent on the promulgation of these ideas to stop. Not only would the cognitive dissonance be too great; the media empire Jones has spent decades building is also entirely premised on these beliefs.[70] The establishment of Jones's fervent base of support and the institutionalization of his ideas via media ventures have made it so that conspiratorial Gnosticism *must* be maintained at all costs for the financial well-being of Jones and his employees, even when those in power make conspiracies mainstream.

## The Ideology of InfoWars

Alex Jones preaches a complicated worldview that combines conspiracies about the JFK assassination with 9/11 trutherism, Obama birtherism, the belief that national governments will soon form a "New World Order," and that mass shootings are engineered by the government using "crisis actors," all sprinkled with a soupçon of paranormalism and Satanic panic. To see if people who buy in to Jones's view of the world share unique social characteristics, as well as how fear and paranormalism relate to this worldview, we created an "InfoWars Ideology" score. As we noted, our 2018 survey asked respondents whether they believed in conspiracies about the New World Order, 9/11, JFK, and mass shootings. We coded these beliefs such that 1 equated to accepting the conspiracy as true and 0 equated to rejecting the conspiracy. We added these four specific beliefs together to create a measure of the worldview Jones espouses.[71] We then examined how a host of factors were related to higher or lower scores on the InfoWars ideology measure. Given Jones's

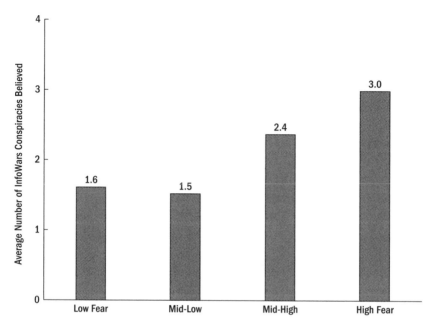

Figure 2.3. Average Score on InfoWars Ideology Count (1–4) by Level of Fear (2018).

obsession with anti-immigration rhetoric, our models also added a xenophobia scale that included levels of agreement with a host of negative statements about immigrants.

The four strongest predictors of holding an InfoWars ideology were (in order) paranormalism, high levels of fear, xenophobia, and the belief that Satan causes evil. As we have found with all conspiracies, fear is tightly bound to the belief that the world is not as it seems (see Figure 2.3). The likelihood of sharing a mind-set with Jones rises significantly as fear increases. Whether Jones is primarily capitalizing on preexisting fear or sowing its seeds, one thing is for certain: Jones benefits handsomely from high levels of fear.

Political conservatism was a significant predictor of InfoWars ideology until we added a measure of xenophobia, which mediated the relationship between conservatism and affinity for the ideas of InfoWars. In other words, political conservatives are more likely to buy into Jones's ideas to the extent that they have high levels of xenophobia.[72] Younger Americans, white people, men, and those with lower levels of education also showed a greater propensity toward the beliefs espoused by In-foWars and Jones. So a young, white, poorly educated, xenophobic man is the prototypical audience member for Jones. It turns out that some things *are* what they seem. Notably, gender was the strongest social characteristic predicting InfoWars beliefs, lending further credence to our analysis of Jones's jeremiads as masculinist hero fantasies.

Looking closely at the InfoWars subculture, we can see how the specific content of particular conspiracy theories points directly to the underlying fears. In the case of the ideology vociferated by Jones, fears about the federal government, foreigners, gun control, and the eclipsing of masculinist power in a multicultural world are all readily apparent. Although believers need not necessarily hold all these fears or ideas simultaneously, they are the basic parameters of the InfoWars worldview.

At the same time, fundamental features of conspiracy theories, such as a conspiratorial Gnosticism that situates believers as heroically wrestling agency from evil agents of control, are also readily apparent. Marty and Jan Dotson, two members of a "Constitutional Community" in Idaho who readily consume InfoWars media, perfectly summarized these features during their interview for the documentary *New World Order*:

> MARTY DOTSON: I wanna be a free man, myself. I wanna be free to live for God, to help my brothers, to have love for one another. I don't wanna be controlled. And I think the New World Order is control. And, is evil, I believe.
>
> JAN DOTSON: There are two forces. There is no grey matter. It's all either black or it's white. It *is* good versus evil. And good will always prevail, because when we know the Truth, the Truth truly will set us free.
>
> MARTY DOTSON: .... If we don't have our own militias, our own groups, and our government comes against us, we're just slaves. They can enslave us or put us in prison, whatever they want to do with us.[73]

## The Age of Conspiracy

Conspiracy theories have always been a fixture of American culture and politics.[74] More generally, conspiracy theories appear to be a basic by-product of the functioning of the human brain under conditions of fear, anxiety, and perceived threat from outside social groups. But while conspiratorial ideologies may be perennial and inevitable, that such views have been recently proliferating in the digital age, and will likely continue expanding into the foreseeable future, is also clear. It seems we are rapidly entering the age of conspiracy, where legitimate sources of information are derided as "fake news" while actual purveyors of fake news such as InfoWars are seen as arbiters of Truth. There are three key reasons for the increasing prevalence of conspiracy theories.

First, increasing diffusion, access to, and frequent use of the new medium of cyberspace create increased social and communicational environments for conspiracy theories to spawn, develop, and spread. In this sense, conspiracy theories are immanently modern.[75] In such open platforms, anyone can say anything, and it can spread "virally," with false and negative stories diffusing much more rapidly and extending much further than true and positive stories.[76] Furthermore, social media use and multitasking also increase anxiety, and anxiety is strongly and positively connected to perceiving and believing conspiracies.[77] Thanks to these advances in communication technology, we are constantly inundated by information not directly connected to our own lives. Anyone plugged into the news or social media is exposed to repeated stories about characters we will never meet, like politicians, the wealthy, and celebrities, and world-shaping events we are not directly involved in, such as legislative disputes, wars, revolutions, and protests around the world, not to mention the latest viral outrage, concern, or triumph spread instantaneously throughout self-selected communication channels and information silos. The people who have the power to influence this world are beyond our means. We never see them in person. We only experience them on screens. They might as well be holograms. We cannot change anything they do. In effect, they are shadowy and operate in secret, at least as far as we are concerned. Conspiracies offer a meaningful way to make sense of these circumstances.

Second, conspiracy theories are likely to proliferate more widely in the United States specifically in response to the changing political and cultural environment of the post-Trump political era. Beyond the furtive commander in chief's frequent espousal of conspiracy theories and his affinity for media outlets such as InfoWars, Trump's brand of politics is built on cynicism about the efficacy of political institutions mixed with populism, both of which are hallmarks of conspiracism.[78] To the extent that Trump's policies and rhetoric increase cynicism about mainstream institutions and encourage populism, conspiracism should increase.

Third and finally, conspiracy theories are likely to thrive in the response to the political economy and military/carceral capacity of the United States in the early twenty-first century. In terms of economics, wealth concentration and social inequality have been increasing sharply in the United States.[79] Changes to social contexts that increase perceptions of threat and insecurity result in higher levels of conspiratorial ideation among resident populations.[80] In conjunction, and reciprocally influencing wealth concentration, changes to the legal and legislative environment have allowed unlimited and opaque financial contributions to political entities and operatives, resulting in "political capture" and disproportionate influence by the wealthy.[81] At the same time, the United States has, by far, the most extensive military capacity and imprisons more of its own citizens than any other country on Earth, to say nothing of increasing levels of surveillance capacity. These facts are indisputable. In such an alienating political, economic, technological, and cultural environment, is the appeal of narratives that preach awareness, autonomy, and agency really any wonder?

3

## Apocalypse How?

*Fear of Natural, Environmental, and Human-Made Disasters*

Fear of natural disasters, climate change, and the end of the world as we know it all figure prominently in the American psyche. From devastating California wildfires to the destruction wrought by hurricanes, natural disasters are a depressingly familiar feature of American life.

Despite the fear that such disasters bring in their wake, for most Americans that fear does not translate into preparedness behaviors. Others, however, break the mold and take preparedness to an extreme. They are ready for just about any man-made environmental disaster or natural disaster and even the Apocalypse—if it comes to that. Known as preppers or survivalists, this group of Americans has a long list of fears, but they are not paralyzed by them.[1] If anything, their fears are energizing. In this chapter, we explore fears of catastrophic disaster and even the end of the world as we know it through the lens of the prepper community to uncover why the same fear leads some people to take protective action for themselves and their families while the majority of Americans take no action at all.

### You're on Your Own

Preparing for the end of the world can be a full-time job. Such is the case for Rick Austen and his wife, who goes by the moniker "Survivor Jane." They live in the Appalachian Mountains, surrounded by a "camouflaged" food forest. To the casual observer, their garden appears to be a useless, overgrown patch of weeds. The couple hopes that after the Shit Hits the Fan (abbreviated SHTF by preppers), hungry marauders will just pass them by, unaware of the bounty hidden in plain sight. The SHTF scenario Rick and Jane fear most is an electromagnetic pulse (EMP) that would fry the electrical grid and render every device with a microchip inoperable. An EMP could be caused by an enemy power exploding a nuclear device in the atmosphere. But, frighteningly, an EMP could have a natural origin as well. In 1859, a powerful solar storm unleashed a coronal mass ejection into Earth's atmosphere, an occurrence known as the Carrington Event. Should such an event occur today, it would have a devastating impact on modern technology. Whatever its origins, an EMP could leave society in near-medieval conditions. Rick and Jane are preparing themselves for what they see as the inevitable.

Many Americans could not imagine a life without smartphones, Netflix, and the Internet; indeed, younger Americans have never known a life without them. But the consequences of an EMP would go far deeper than destroying our ability to entertain ourselves and communicate with one another. Absent mass production, everything from food to medicine to clothing will become increasingly difficult to find as existing supplies diminish. Survivor Jane is thinking ahead about one modern necessity— toilet paper. As she discusses on her Survivor Jane website,

> As most of you who know of me, you know I'm a girlie-girl and will try my darnedest to find out what I can do to stay a girlie-girl when the poo-hits-the-fan. Not gonna catch me with my pants down . . . well you might but I'll have a clean fanny! *grin* . . .
>
> I really did my research on this subject—the toilet paper alternative query. I just didn't want to wait until things got worse to find an alternative—or be forced to find one. And, I couldn't see having huge stock piles of TP that would one day disappear and I would still be up poo's creek.[2]

Thankfully Jane has found an alternative—her own invention:

> The reveal—drum roll please. A simple 1 gallon garden sprayer I purchased for $9!
> Wait. . . . wait! Before saying anything—hear me out.
> I cut 4.5–5 inches off the wand to shorten it.

> Then I placed the remaining wand (the part that connects to the tank) in boiling water to soften it to make a "hook-shape" (the hook shape makes

it gender friendly for those hard to reach areas due to obstacles some of us have (grin).)

And—whaa-laa a bidet with a control for a light misting to a full-on power blast. I call it The Hiney-Hydrant.™³

Given the ingenuity displayed by Rick and Jane, it is not surprising that the couple is committed to teaching others about the prepper lifestyle. Survival is now their business. They sell preparedness books and offer tutorials through their websites. They have also recently started an annual camp for preppers just outside the scenic mountain town of Saluda, North Carolina, in the Blue Ridge Mountains.

*** 

I (Ann) attended the inaugural Prepper Camp in 2014 with my sister and an undergraduate researcher.[4] Preppers came from all over the United States to attend the camp, and they brought with them a wide range of fears that motivated their lifestyle.

The most widely shared fear was of an EMP attack, and this was the subject of a talk given under a big tent by William Forstchen, author of the wildly popular book *One Second After*,[5] which tells the story of the struggle to survive in a small North Carolina town after the United States is attacked with an EMP weapon, leaving the country without electricity. Although a work of fiction, the book had a powerful influence, even being cited during a congressional hearing as lawmakers sought to understand and defend against the possibility of a real-life attack.[6]

Although EMPs played a prominent role at Prepper Camp, attendees are very accepting of others' fears, even if they aren't particularly concerned with that specific disaster themselves. For example, on learning that my sister lives in Utah, a prepper named "John," who hails from the southern United States, earnestly asked about her plans in the event of a supervolcano eruption in Yellowstone.[7] Another attendee shared that she had survived Hurricane Katrina in New Orleans. The trauma and terror of that event caused her to become a serious prepper. A couple from Ohio, who brought their kids along, see prepping as a lifestyle and were concerned with a wide variety of SHTF scenarios, including economic collapse and EMPs.

Other commonly discussed scenarios included economic collapse, catastrophic natural disasters, and terrorism. To prepare for these possibilities, we participated in a wide array of demonstrations and classes, as preppers shared their expertise with one another. All the skills we learned were designed to help preppers live self-sufficiently and without the need for grocery stores, hospitals, and other institutions that wouldn't be available after the SHTF. We spent time in the woods foraging for wild edibles. We learned disaster medical procedures from a paramedic turned prepper who goes by the name Skinny Medic. He pointed out that you never know when you might be the first responder and that medical services as we know them might not be available after the SHTF. Beekeeping was quite popular (until some bees got out, causing a bit of an uproar). We also learned blacksmithing on the cheap, archery, food storage techniques, self-defense, how to make snares, and ballistic home defense, among other things that might come in handy should society collapse. The schedule for the most recent Prepper Camp (as of this writing) provided classes on everything from raising rabbits, canning, and home brewing to the importance of stockpiling gold and silver, assessing possible threats to one's homestead, and selecting the proper firearms.[8]

Personal survival is not the only issue discussed at Prepper Camp. There were serious debates about how to handle the "golden horde," refugees from the cities who would swarm farms and small towns when the SHTF, or your neighbors who had failed to prepare. Discussions about whether to help them or turn them away (or worse) became animated at times. Underlying all the discussion, however, was total agreement in the prepper community that Americans are simply not ready for the next catastrophic disaster.

## American Disaster in the Making

Developing an active prepper lifestyle is, no doubt, too extreme of a response to fears about disasters for most of us. However, the assessment by preppers about the general level of disaster preparedness in America is fairly accurate; we are not ready. The Chapman Survey of American Fears (CSAF) found that only 30 percent of Americans have a basic emergency kit as recommended by the Federal Emergency Management Agency (FEMA) and the Red Cross, although 83 percent believe such

TABLE 3.1. Disaster Preparedness in America (2018).

| Preparedness | Total | Northeast | Midwest | South | West |
|---|---|---|---|---|---|
| Emergency Kit—Yes | 30% | 18% | 31% | 26% | 42% |
| Emergency Plan—Yes | 36% | 31% | 36% | 35% | 40% |
| Improved chance of surviving with a kit | 83% | 76% | 79% | 85% | 88% |

Source: CSAF (2018).
Note: N = 1,190.

a kit, with food, water, and medicine, would improve their chances of surviving a disaster (see Table 3.1). Only 36 percent have made any kind of emergency plans for themselves and their households.

This lack of preparedness does not reflect a lack of concern about disasters. Many Americans share the fears of the prepper community about catastrophic hurricanes (33 percent), the power grid collapsing (39 percent), pandemics (39 percent), drought (38 percent), floods (31 percent), tornadoes (35 percent), blizzards (27 percent), and even volcanic eruptions (19 percent; see Table 3.2). And it is not as if Americans' fears about disasters are entirely disconnected from reality. Americans' fears about disaster are regionally appropriate. As one might expect, earthquake fears are highest in the West (46 percent), whereas fear of hurricanes is highest in the South (48 percent) and Northeast (37 percent) but quite low in the Midwest (12 percent).

Americans do worry about the fury of nature, but they are equally afraid of what people can do. Among the most feared disasters are human-made disasters such as financial collapse (49 percent), nuclear weapons attack (43 percent), and biological warfare (45 percent).

So how do Americans explain their lack of preparedness when it is clear that they are very afraid? They have many excuses it seems. More than half of Americans believe that emergency responders will come to their aid (51 percent). Other explanations include feeling like they do not have enough time (40 percent). A third, 33 percent, just do not want to think about it. For 28 percent, the problem is simply not knowing what they should do.

Unfortunately, the expectation that first responders will arrive in the aftermath of a major disaster is unrealistic. Some disasters are just too large and overwhelm local services. For example, the EF5 tornado that

TABLE 3.2. Fear of Disasters (2018).

| Natural Disasters | Total | Northeast | Midwest | South | West |
|---|---|---|---|---|---|
| Pandemic or Epidemic | 39% | 43% | 30% | 40% | 38% |
| Devastating Drought | 38% | 43% | 26% | 35% | 46% |
| Devastating Tornado | 35% | 29% | 42% | 42% | 20% |
| Devastating Earthquake | 31% | 25% | 20% | 28% | 46% |
| Devastating Flood | 31% | 29% | 24% | 36% | 28% |
| Devastating Hurricane | 33% | 37% | 12% | 48% | 21% |
| Devastating Blizzard | 27% | 39% | 33% | 23% | 20% |
| Devastating Volcanic Eruption | 19% | 18% | 13% | 18% | 21% |
| Man-Made Disasters | Total | Northeast | Midwest | South | West |
| Biological Warfare | 45% | 49% | 42% | 46% | 45% |
| Financial Collapse | 49% | 54% | 47% | 50% | 47% |
| Nuclear Weapon Attack | 43% | 50% | 39% | 44% | 39% |
| Electrical Grid Collapse | 39% | 46% | 37% | 37% | 38% |

Source: Chapman University Survey of American Fears (2018).
Note: N = 1,190. Values shown are the percentages of respondents who reported being afraid or very afraid of each phenomenon.

devastated Joplin, Missouri, in 2011 left 158 dead, more than 1,000 people injured, and 7,000 homes destroyed. Even with massive efforts from first responders all over the region, it took days to bring help to those affected by the disaster. This is why the Red Cross and FEMA both recommend having supplies such as food, water, and medicine that will sustain a household for at least 72 hours following a disaster. Many emergency managers recommend supplies to last even longer than that. Beyond these basics, preparations should take into account that services such as electricity, gas, water, sewage treatment, and telephones may be cut off for days or even a week or longer during a disaster. A supply kit is essential to manage during these outages. It took New York more than two weeks to restore power to 95 percent of the 8.5 million people left in the dark after Superstorm Sandy hit the Eastern Seaboard. Four months after Hurricane Maria hit Puerto Rico, half a million people were still without power, and many on the island had no reliable water source.[9] This type of months-long (or longer) scenario is exactly what preppers have in mind when they assess their own readiness for a disaster.

Preppers have great respect for first responders, police, and military. Indeed, many preppers have served in the military or worked in emergency services. But they scoff at the idea that anyone will be there to rescue you in a catastrophe. Their slogan is "You're on your own," abbreviated YOYO. For a prepper, YOYO boils down to beans, bullets, and bandages. This is shorthand for food, water, medical supplies, and the means to defend oneself and one's stored supplies, also called "preps." Importantly, they emphasize acquiring the skill set to take care of oneself and household beyond laying in supplies.

This philosophy of self-reliance and self-efficacy is an important reason that preppers, despite having a vast array of fears, are actually quite confident about their chances of surviving, or even thriving, post-SHTF. That is, they may fear an EMP but are quite prepared for it to happen. Some preppers even welcome a smallish disaster from time to time to test their preparedness and use their preps.

## Climate Change and Environmental Fears

Hurricanes Harvey, Irma, and Rita broke records for the destruction they wrought and contributed to the "single-most powerful month ever recorded in the Atlantic in terms of hurricane intensity."[10] The ferocity of Hurricane Irma stoked fears that this might be a new "normal" due to climate change. Miami mayor Tomás Regalado, a Republican, told reporters, "This is the time to talk about climate change. This is the time that the president and the E.P.A. and whoever makes decisions needs to talk about climate change . . . If this isn't climate change, I don't know what is. This is a truly, truly poster child for what is to come."[11]

The mayor of Miami's assertion is backed by a number of studies. For example, research shows that 500-year floods could become 24-year events. One study concluded that "projected sea-level rise leads to large increases in future overall flood heights associated with tropical cyclones in New York City."[12] The scientists used historical flooding in New Jersey and New York plus sophisticated global climate modeling to study how often cyclone-driven floods occurred and how severe they were. "People may be thinking Sandy was a once-in-a-generation event. If you say to them it's going to happen multiple times in a generation, that makes a big impact, and will hopefully get people to start saying we must mitigate to delay this."[13]

The memory of Hurricane Sandy's destructive force is still quite relevant here. Given Sandy's destructive 80- to 115-mile-per-hour winds, felt over a 1,100-mile area, and with storm surges over 13 feet in places like Battery Park, this warning should not be ignored.[14] Despite the Trump administration's denials of climate change, scientists are making advances every day in explaining not only the nature of climate change but also the very real impact on disasters. Even a decade ago, one did not find a lot of support for the idea that climate change could be linked to particular weather-related disasters. That is changing. According to *Scientific American,*

> The breakthrough paper took the existing science a step further. Using a climate model, the researchers compared simulations accounting for climate change with scenarios in which human-caused global warming did not exist. They found that the influence of climate change roughly doubled the risk of an individual heat wave. The key to the breakthrough was framing the question in the right way—not asking whether climate change "caused" the event, but how much it might have affected the risk of it occurring at all.[15]

Thus, climate change is now implicated in the increasing severity of droughts, wildfires, heat waves, and hurricanes. To be sure, scientists remain cautious about claims that any given weather event was caused primarily by climate change. Nevertheless, consensus is building that climate change's role cannot be ignored and must be considered in city planning and national preparedness. Reuters noted that the U.S. military was preparing plans of its own: "Nearly half of U.S. military sites are threatened by wild weather linked to climate change, according to a Pentagon study whose findings run contrary to White House views on global warming."[16]

Climate change is not normally a concern of the prepper community. At least it wasn't back in 2014. Most preppers in Saluda were of a decidedly conservative mind-set. But, with the election of Trump and fears of a looming "Trumpocalypse," self-identified liberal preppers have gained attention. As Mac Slavo observes on the popular prepping SHTFPlan website, in a post titled "Liberal Preppers Ready for the Trumpocalypse: 'Tired of Being Seen as Wusses Who Won't Survive SHTF,'"

> While many conservative and libertarian-minded preppers may not agree AT ALL on their previous support for Hillary Clinton, or their anger and hate of Trump, they have to concede that a new wave of "liberal preppers" may be quite right in preparing for the likelihood of collapse or martial law in the years ahead. The potential for government overreach or rebellion among the population is very high in the next four years . . . it is only a matter of waiting for the pretext of crisis.[17]

Perhaps liberal oriented preppers have always been there in the overlapping space occupied by survivalists who favor renewable energy and sustainability for off-grid homesteading and their green living progressive counterparts. In recognition of the intersection of interests, many prepper expo events are branded as "Survival and Green Living" or "Crisis Preparation and Sustainable Living."[18] Preppers also eschew chemical fertilizers and pesticides, and are very concerned with water quality and pollution. As we shall see, fears over water pollution, air pollution, and climate change are broadly shared by Americans beyond preppers.

## Increasing Fear

In the last several years, the brief span of time between 2016 and 2018, we have witnessed sharply increasing fears about environmental issues (see Figure 3.1).

In 2018, several pollution-related concerns appeared in our top 10 list of American fears, likely due to fears about policy changes in Washington. The Trump administration has charted a drastically different path, ordering the U.S. Environmental Protection Agency not to enforce major pollution laws and firing the entire Science Advisory Board of the Environmental Protection Agency (EPA).[19] Water pollution is a big source of anxiety, with a majority of Americans, some 62 percent, saying they fear pollution of "oceans, rivers and streams." This is up sharply from the previous year's total of 54 percent.

The fact that water pollution has become such a prominent fear in 2018 may be related to the reversal of environmental policies of the

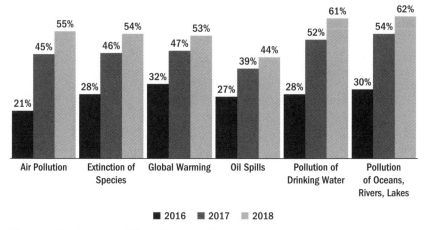

Figure 3.1. Environmental Fears (2016–2018).

Obama administration. One of Donald Trump's first actions as president was to withdraw the EPA's "Waters of the United States" rule. This action drastically reduced the number of rivers and streams that could be protected from agricultural runoff under the Clean Water Act. Another of the administration's first actions was to withdraw the "Stream Buffer" rule, which had been enacted to protect Appalachian rivers and streams from strip mining.[20]

Along with water pollution in general, fears over what comes out of the tap have also seen a jump. Some 61 percent of Americans fear for the quality of their drinking water. This should not be a surprise, considering the prominent news coverage of lead poisoning in the drinking water of Flint, Michigan, as well as the subsequent discovery of contaminated drinking water in other communities around the country.[21] The prominence of these fears is consistent with years of public opinion polling, which show that water pollution typically outranks other environmental problems in the mind of the public. Water pollution ranks second overall, followed closely by drinking water quality.

In addition to water concerns, there was also an increase in the percentage of Americans who say they fear climate change, 53 percent, up from 47 percent the year before, and air pollution at 55 percent, up from 45 percent. These are the ninth and seventh greatest fears, respectively, as measured by the CSAF in 2018. The sharp rise in the number of

Americans who now say that they fear climate change (and air pollution, which contributes to climate change) may be linked to Trump's controversial decision to withdraw from the Paris Climate Accord. Moreover, climate change was treated as a national security issue under the Obama administration, a policy that was reversed by President Trump.[22]

Public opinion polls show that climate change ranks lower than most other environmental issues as a source of public concern.[23] This is likely due to the perception that the effects of the warming oceans and atmosphere are remote, far in the future, and more likely to affect "other people." What is striking about these environmental fears, including water pollution and drinking water quality, is that they figure more prominently among Americans' top fears in 2018 than ever before, but the fear is focused on local issues rather than global consequences. This does not mean, however, that Americans do not fear global catastrophe.

## Apocalypse How?

Humans have long feared the end is nigh. From the Greeks to the Romans, Islam to Christianity, end-times narratives are built into the foundation of many religions.[24] In the United States, a particular strain of Christian apocalyptic thinking that combines the fevered dreams of the Bible's book of Revelation with later theological developments such as the Rapture and guessing games about the identity of the Antichrist has become exceptionally popular.[25] Consider Tim LaHaye and Jerry Jenkin's Left Behind series, which unfolds a narrative about a war with Satan and the Antichrist that occurs in the aftermath of the Rapture. Sales for the entire Left Behind series are estimated to be more than 63 million.[26] Thinking one knows the nature of the Apocalypse seems to compel believers to specify the date when it will occur.[27] The Millerites and Jehovah's Witnesses were well known for their failed attempts at naming the date of our ends.[28] More recently, religious broadcaster Harold Camping caused much excitement, followed by great disappointment, when he predicted that the world would end on May 21, 2011 . . . and then on October 21 . . . followed by an apology on October 22.[29] Even more recently, a prophecy dubiously based on the Mayan calendar predicted the end of the world on December 21, 2012.[30]

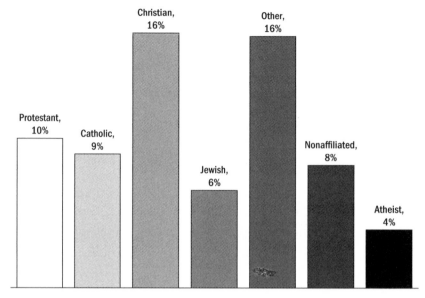

Figure 3.2. Percentage Who Believe "the World Will End in My Lifetime" by Religious Tradition (2016).

Despite the fact that prophecies about the end of the world have a 100 percent failure rate, they remain a part of the American identity. In 2016, we asked our survey respondents for their views on a series of statements about the possible end of the world. Fully 13 percent of Americans believed that the world will end in their lifetimes. The importance of Christianity to American end-times thinking is also apparent. Fully one half of the sample believe that the world will end as outlined in the Christian Bible.

However, assuming that American pessimism about the world's future is confined to the religious would be a mistake. Figure 3.2 breaks down the belief that the "world will end in my lifetime" by religious tradition. For certain, religious Americans are more likely to believe that the world will end in their lifetimes. Ten percent of Protestants, 9 percent of Catholics, and 16 percent of those who are Christians but refuse the labels of Protestant or Catholic (or do not know that they are, in fact, Protestants) think the end of the world is nigh. Jews are more skeptical of such claims, with only 6 percent expressing such belief. Americans of

TABLE 3.3. Fear of the End of the World.

| Fear of the end of the world | Americans who responded "afraid" or "very afraid" |
|---|---|
| The world will end within my lifetime | 13% |
| The world will end as outlined in the Bible | 50% |
| The world will end due to a world war | 25% |
| The world will end due to a man-made environmental disaster | 32% |
| The world will end due to a natural disaster | 36% |

Source: CSAF (2016).
Note: N = 1,511.

other faiths, including Muslims, Buddhists, and the panoply of smaller faiths in the United States are also swayed by apocalyptic claims, with 16 percent believing in an imminent end of days. But even the nonreligious are represented as well. Eight percent of those who claim no religion, and 4 percent of atheists think the world will end before (or perhaps we should say the same time as) they die.

Americans seem to have a minor fascination with the end of the world, whether religious or not. Thankfully our culture has provided a host of secular Armageddons from which to choose. From scientific warnings about global climate catastrophe to the Ebola panic and supervolcanoes, the world as we know it seems perched on a knife's edge. When considering what will bring about the Apocalypse, many Americans believe it will take the form of a human-made environmental disaster such as global warming (32 percent). More than a third (36 percent) believe that a natural disaster such as a supervolcano or an asteroid striking the planet will bring our end. A fourth of Americans (25 percent) think that a world war will bring the Apocalypse (see Table 3.3).

Doomsday preppers, naturally, envisage a coming apocalypse of some sort. At prepper camp, the leading contender for the cause was an EMP attack by terrorists or other hostile foreign power. Many believed in a biblical end to the world, but religious belief was not a requirement of attendance. The concern for an EMP-driven apocalypse is a modern update to the Cold War nuclear annihilation fears. The difference between preppers who fear the end and others in America is that preppers plan to survive and even thrive in a postapocalyptic hellscape. As Danile Wojcik observes,

> most hard-core survivalists have "given up" on a corrupt society that they consider to be doomed. Although human action is regarded as futile in averting catastrophes and saving society, personal salvation is possible through self-sufficiency, retreatism, and the development of certain pre-scribed skills and behaviors. The feelings of powerlessness otherwise evoked by fears of nuclear annihilation and other imminent disasters are displaced by elaborate preparations that provide the hope of surviving doomsday . . .[31]

The feeling of control in an otherwise uncontrollable situation is the key to fear reduction for preppers. A lack of control, as we have seen, is a key driver of fear across a broad list of domains. To regain a sense of control then, preppers believe they

> must rely on their own skill resourcefulness, and rugged individualism to endure societal destruction. The majority of survivalists seem to embrace the fatalistic view that nuclear war and other cataclysms are inevitable, envisioning themselves as post-apocalyptic pioneers who will be the dominant inhabitants of a devastated new frontier and who will gradu-ally rebuild society from the ruins.[32]

This confidence in one's own abilities, combined with extensive prep-aration, allows the prepping community to turn their fears into a pro-ductive vision of the future, however bleak it may be.

Preppers are well aware that their activities are viewed as extreme by mainstream society and tend to only discuss prepping among them-selves. But with the Doomsday Clock, maintained by the members of the Bulletin of the Atomic Scientists, set at two minutes to midnight due to the "looming threats of nuclear war and climate change," I can't help but recall the words of one prepper: "Am I crazy, or are you?"[33]

4

# Beyond Contagion

*Terrorism, the Media, and Public Fear*

The atmosphere was festive for the annual Christmas party and meetings taking place at the Inland Regional Center in San Bernardino, California. Hal Houser was at the meeting and recalled it was very much like previous years. Co-workers mingled, had discussions, and posed for pictures. But this would not be an ordinary day. Instead, the party would turn into a deadly terror attack that left 14 people dead and 22 others wounded. Houser described what happened:

> There were . . . about 12 or 13 of us gathered around the tree to pose for the Christmas picture. As we're starting to jockey for positions and get into shape, we hear some loud bangs outside. My initial thought was, you know, "Wow. Awful close. What's going on?" And this black-clad figure started shooting. We were sitting ducks. He raked from [the] end of the building all the way down to where he ran out of bullets at the middle of the Christmas tree photo. I was to the left. The three gentlemen on the right side were all killed. He ran out of bullets and was very clumsily taking out his first magazine to reload and at that time, what turned out to be, later on, the wife, came through and started shooting towards the back tables . . .[1]

After many people had been shot, the shooters went through the room, aiming under the tables, spraying bullets to get anyone who was still alive or playing dead. The first officer on scene, Lieutenant Mike Madden, arrived 3.5 minutes after the call went out.[2] With the quick arrival of two more officers, the team went in to clear the building and confront the shooters, not knowing they had just fled the scene. The 22 wounded who were rushed to the hospital all survived thanks to the efforts of first responders.

Local and national television stations broadcast updates on San Bernardino minute to minute. In a press conference carried live on TV, police told the public that the shooters had escaped in a "dark-colored SUV." Earlier that morning, a black SUV making an abrupt lane change had caught the attention of Stewart Boden, who took note of the license plate.[3] It wasn't until he got home and saw the news reports that he realized the connection and called 911. The information he provided, together with survivor accounts, was crucial in helping the police locate the killers. In this instance, media coverage helped police locate the terrorists.

Similarly, live wall-to-wall coverage played a role in locating the so-called Chelsea bomber, who had been at large for two days after planting bombs at a five-kilometer race and a train station in New Jersey and more in the Chelsea neighborhood of Manhattan. Three of the bombs detonated, causing injuries to 31 people but no fatalities. A bar owner, who had been watching CNN coverage of the bombings, recognized the suspect from the news reports when he saw a man sleeping in the doorway to his bar and called 911.[4]

Although the news media has assisted law enforcement in their hunt for terrorists in cases such as these, there is also a darker and more insidious impact of this coverage. There is broad consensus among researchers and law enforcement that media attention fuels terrorism and mass shootings. Indeed, the Pulse nightclub shooter checked for his press coverage *during* the rampage in which he killed 49 people and wounded 53 others in Orlando, Florida. Another shooter, who killed 32 and wounded 17 at Virginia Tech, "interrupted his killing spree to mail a videotape to NBC to claim credit and explain his motives."[5] The sick symbiotic relationship between the media and terrorists has long been recognized. Margaret Thatcher observed in 1985 that "we must try to find ways to starve the terrorist and the hijacker of the oxygen of publicity on which they depend."[6] Thatcher's observation clearly remains relevant today. Terrorists can expect to receive extensive coverage for their attacks, thereby spreading their ideas, along with images of terror and fear worldwide. Furthermore, empirical evidence supports Thatcher's observation. The number and severity of terrorist attacks increase with increased press coverage.[7] But media outlets profit from such coverage. Indeed, coverage of the Paris terror attacks in 2015 yielded a significant ratings boost for both CNN and Fox News in the United States. Both had their highest ratings of the year, with the exception of the presidential debates.[8]

Mass shootings that are not labeled "terrorism" are also fueled by media coverage. Studies have empirically demonstrated these "contagion" effects. For example, following the mass shootings at Columbine High school, in which 12 students and a teacher died and 21 others were wounded, attention became focused on the potential for copycat crimes spurred on by media coverage. Law enforcement and school officials saw spikes in threats of violence in school districts across the country. Researchers in Pennsylvania estimated that such copycat threats peaked 10 days after the Columbine shootings.[9] But not only threats follow a widely publicized shooting. Scholars have also shown a contagion effect on violence, such that mass killings are more likely to occur within two weeks of another incident.[10]

Similar to the idea of contagion but broader in scope, "generalized imitation" may be a better way to conceptualize how and why mass killers influence one another:

> Generalized imitation is the learned ability to perform behaviors that are similar to behaviors observed or described, even when performance is delayed . . . Generalized imitation does not suggest that a person will always perform an exact copy of the model's behavior; rather, it suggests that the person will perform a behavior with similar characteristics.[11]

The key point is that a copycat incident need not be exact, and the imitation may be removed in time from the original. Investigators often find that mass shooters reference killings that occurred months, years, or even decades prior.

The impact of Columbine continues today. Two decades after the killings, a fascination with the shooters remains. For example, in 2018 two high school students from Adair County High School in Columbia, Kentucky, dressed as the Columbine shooters for Halloween and took photos of themselves at school, reenacting some parts of the incident. The girls then posted pictures of their reenactments, along with actual photos from 1999 to their social media accounts. Both were suspended from school.[12] Similarly, in the dark corners of the Internet, where the rage of would-be killers festers, the Columbine shooters and other mass murderers are adored as celebrities. Killers such as the Virginia Tech shooter and the Sandy Hook killer directly referenced Columbine and appeared to have made a study of prior mass killings.[13] Similarly, over the course of a few months,

> The shooter at Umpqua Community College in Oregon in October 2015 mentioned as an inspiration the man who killed a television reporter and cameraman in Roanoke, Virginia, and posted the video to Facebook in August of that year. That Roanoke killer mentioned the white suprema-cist shooter who killed congregants at an African-American church in Charleston, South Carolina, two months before.[14]

Whether through contagion or a more generalized imitation effect, that mass killers and those who may be considering committing violent acts are studying previous attacks by using overly detailed media reports is clear.[15] These accounts not only serve as a do-it-yourself guide for aspir-ing killers but tend to glorify the act as well. Potential killers thereby see their violent fantasies as a path to fame.

Broadcast media are not the sole problem, as was the case in Marga-ret Thatcher's era. The roles of the Internet and social media have come under scrutiny for their contribution to radicalizing would-be terror-ists. Indeed, families of some of the San Bernardino victims filed a law-suit alleging that "without defendants Twitter, Facebook and Google (YouTube), the explosive growth of ISIS [the Islamic State of Iraq and Syria] over the last few years into the most feared terrorist group in the world would not have been possible."[16] Online terrorist propaganda also played a role in the radicalization of the Orlando shooter, according to the Federal Bureau of Investigation (FBI). Survivors and victims' fami-lies filed a lawsuit against Twitter, Facebook, and Google in this case as well. Their suit alleges "that ISIS members and its official news outlets use numerous accounts . . . [to] publish the organization's messages and to recruit and 'radicalize' persons," such as the Orlando shooter.[17]

The role of extensive media coverage in cases of terrorism and mass murder is complex. In some cases, news coverage was the crucial link between law enforcement and the public. At the same time, extensive media coverage of mass violence contributes to the generation of future attacks by providing terrorists and shooters with a platform for their views, as well as through contagion, imitation, and radicalization effects. But a "second stage" effect of media coverage of terrorism and mass murder also often goes unnoticed, namely, the media's effect on fear about these events, as well as on those stereotyped as being associated with terrorism. These second-stage effects are what we wanted to study with our fear surveys. We first used data from our surveys to see whether and how media coverage reinforces and heightens public fears about terrorism and mass shootings.

## Media Consumption and Fear of Terrorism and Mass Murder

As we noted in Chapter 1, the human brain is wired to hone in on threats, especially novel and scary situations. This "increased anxiety stops ongoing activity and orients attention to the threatening appearance so that learning can take place."[18] Knowledge about and, especially, images of a terror attack or mass shooting engage the brain's surveillance system, causing us to pay close attention to this coverage as we seek to learn more about the threat. All this extra attention leads to a ratings boost for the media, but paying close attention to media coverage of terrorism and mass shootings also increases the public's fears about such events. We found widespread fear among Americans about being the victim of a mass shooting (42 percent) or a terror attack (40 percent). These fears are indeed significantly affected by patterns of media consumption.

Previous research has found that watching local TV news tends to increase the fear of crime due to graphic and even gruesome video, whereas newspaper readers do not appear to have an increased fear of crime.[19] Similarly, we find that mass shooting fears are significantly higher, on average, among viewers of both local TV and cable news. Viewers of both CNN and Fox News were more likely to fear being the victim of a mass or random shooting, even when controlling for the effects of social and religious characteristics, as well as political partisanship. Viewers of daytime talk shows, which often feature crime victims as guests, were similarly more likely to be afraid of becoming the victim of a mass shooting. People who regularly got their news from social media sites like Facebook and Twitter also had significantly higher fears about mass shootings. Fears about being the victim of terrorism show similar patterns. Regular viewers of Fox News, local news, and daytime talk shows all had significantly more fear of terrorism, as did people who regularly got their news through social media.

Fears of terrorism are not confined to our television sets, iPads, and the Twitter feeds on our smartphones, however. For example, 24 percent of our respondents said that they have avoided going to concerts, sporting events, or other public venues, because of fears about terrorism. Some 53 percent of Americans said that they fear traveling abroad because of recent acts of terror, and 70 percent believe they would be targeted by terrorists if they did travel outside of the United States. Not surprisingly then, 78 percent are willing to put up with longer lines for security screenings at the airport, because of the feared threat of terrorism. Avoiding public spaces for fear of terror attacks is similar to withdrawing from public spaces due to crime, which we discuss in Chapter 5.

In addition to media effects, there were also strong and significant gender effects in fear of terrorism and mass shootings, even when controlling for media usage, social characteristics, and political ideology. As noted in Chapter 1, vulnerability theory provides an explanation for why women are more likely to express fears of being the victim of violence than are men. Fears about being the victim of a terror attack or a mass shooting appear to be another manifestation of overall social vulnerability. However, that women are also specifically targeted by some rampage killers is worth noting. This was the case with the Toronto killer who plowed his rental van into a crowded sidewalk, killing 10 and injuring 15. Prior to the killing, he posted this to his Facebook page:

> "Private (Recruit) Minassian Infantry 00010, wishing to speak to Sgt. 4chan please. C23249161," reads the post. "The Incel Rebellion has already begun! We will overthrow all the Chads and Stacys! All hail the Supreme Gentleman [previous incel killer]."[20]

The term *incel* is shorthand for "involuntary celibate" and refers to an ideology grounded in misogyny that is "predicated on the notion that feminism has ruined society, therefore there is a need for a 'gender revolt' in order to reclaim a particular type of manhood based on both male and white superiority."[21] Men who identify as incels believe that they are entitled to sex and are deeply resentful of men and women who they see as socially "normal" and attractive, dubbing them "Chads," "Stacys," and "normies." Many incels posted celebratory messages after a 22-year-old man killed 6 people and injured 14 others in Isla Vista, California, near the University of California, Santa Barbara, campus. He became a "hero" to incels because he posted a video to YouTube explaining that the killings were meant to punish women for sexual rejection and the sexually active men of whom he was jealous. The video, together with his 107-page manifesto, in which he lamented being a virgin, saying, "I'm the perfect guy and yet you throw yourselves at these obnoxious men instead of me, the supreme gentleman," earned him the moniker "Supreme Gentleman" from the online incel community.[22] It was this man to whom the Toronto killer referred just before launching his attack.

Incels took to the Internet to express their approval of the actions of the Toronto killer. They

> cheered the fact that [he] killed more people than [the Isla Vista killer]. A person with the username Letting Go opined that the women of Toronto deserved what they got, "As someone who visited Toronto at the beginning of the month, I can see how a man from that city could be driven to kill a bunch of people like that. The women up there are HORRIBLE— even the ethnic women. It would brighten my day if the majority of the victims were young cunts like the ones that I encountered on my trip."[23]

This incel subculture began to receive widespread media attention following these killings and, as with previous mass murders, an unfortunate level of notoriety. Violent expressions of hypermasculinity in response to perceived emasculation is clearly evident in "incel" terrorists, and these issues are also often an important component of mass school shootings.[24]

## Denying Killers Notoriety

The goal for mass shooters such as incels or school shooters is often notoriety, and thus, the #NoNotoriety movement was born in response.[25] Just as terrorists seek media attention for their attacks, so, too, do many responsible for mass shootings fantasize about going down in history, along with the murderers they idolize.[26] Criminologists Adam Lankford and Eric Madfis argue that the news media should not name or use photos of perpetrators. Nor should previous killers be named or their photos broadcast.[27] They make a compelling case for changing the pattern of media coverage in this way. We have followed suit and not named terrorists or mass shooters here. Denying the shooters and bombers the notoriety they seek is an important step in addressing the threat of contagion and generalized imitation effects.

Founders of the #NoNotoriety movement, whose loved ones died in the Aurora, Colorado, theater shooting, note that it is appropriate to use the perpetrator's name and photo if it assists law enforcement in finding and arresting the shooter. Beyond that, "Notoriety serves as not only a reward for these murderers, but also as a 'call to action' for other like-minded individuals who seek to gain a similar amount of publicity, motivating them to create and carry out copycat acts."[28] The FBI, in conjunction with Texas State University, has a similar campaign that urges law enforcement officers who may be making public statements, along with the press, to avoid naming the perpetrators.[29] Then-FBI director James Comey said after the Pulse nightclub massacre, "You will notice that I am not using the killer's name. And I will try not to do that. Part of what motivates sick people to do this kind of thing is some twisted notion of fame or glory, and I don't want to be part of that for the sake of the victims and their families and so that other twisted minds don't think that this is a path to fame and recognition."[30]

One journalist who has followed the No Notoriety campaign's guidelines is CNN's Anderson Cooper. While in Orlando, covering the Pulse attack, he said that he would not name the shooter and, instead, told viewers, "In the next two hours we want to try to keep the focus where we think it belongs, on the people whose lives were cut short." Cooper then made an emotional seven-minute tribute to the victims.[31] However, some news media, CNN and Cooper included, have made a distinction between lone gunmen mass murderers and terrorists.[32] In covering the San Bernardino attack, all the news networks named both shooters and showed their pictures on what seemed like an endless loop. In explaining why its coverage of apparent lone gunman and terror attacks differs, CNN said,

> Things were a bit different in our coverage last week because very early on it was clear this shooting could be an act of terrorism, which is different

than the shootings we've seen in the past of lone gunman in many cases just looking to kill and for personal notoriety. As an act of terror, there are questions of associates and possible cells, so showing pictures and naming names is important in that regard as it might help law enforcement. So that's the distinction/why we showed the pictures. And even then we try to be judicious in how often we use the picture and the name. Once the investigation seems to have run its course in these types of circumstances then we stop using picture and name. For instance now that the ringleader of the Paris attacks is dead, Anderson has stopped using his name. The 8th terrorist is still on the loose so we use the name and show his picture.[33]

Although media producers claim that the use of terrorists' names and pictures is "judicious," viewers of cable news would have a difficult time escaping that content. Moreover, the San Bernardino shooters' names and photos continued to be used on all the national networks, cable news, and local affiliates long after law enforcement needed assistance. Given that the relationship between terrorists and media coverage is just as detrimental as that between mass shooters and media coverage (and sometimes the two categories overlap), avoiding naming them as well, if at all possible, makes sense. Indeed, because many terrorist attacks are undertaken by self-radicalized individuals rather than directed by terrorist organizations, contagion and imitation effects are quite relevant to terrorist attacks as well.

In addition to withholding names and pictures, scholars have suggested that the news media refrain from giving highly detailed descriptions of shooters' manifestos, grievances, or reasons. Thus, media descriptions of "a purported motive for the shooting . . . may inadvertently be pointing out similarities between the shooter and others that may have otherwise gone unnoticed."[34] Whether an attack is linked to terrorism or not, the news media should avoid amplifying the perpetrators' views or inadvertently glorifying their actions. For our part as viewers, we must become aware of our role as the audience and resist tuning in, despite our fears (and our overstimulated amygdalae) urging us to do so. Better yet, we can let media outlets know that they will not get our attention and the ratings they seek if they continue patterns of irresponsible coverage. We can tweet our displeasure and tune out. Only such a collective revolt of media consumption will change the deleterious coverage of terrorism and mass murder. Ratings dictate content, after all. By continuing to provide the audience and ratings for sensationalistic coverage, we are letting our fears get the better of us and are further perpetuating the very thing we wish to stop.

## Who Are "the Terrorists"?

In addition to fueling imitation and contagion, press coverage and media consumption also frame *who* the public should fear. In our survey, we asked respondents how afraid they were about a variety of extremist groups that potentially posed a threat to society. Media usage patterns played an important role in the groups that different Americans fear.[35] For example, Fox News viewers were more fearful of Islamic extremists, extreme animal-rights groups, and extreme environmentalists while notably exhibiting a lower likelihood of fear about white supremacists and extreme anti-immigration groups. CNN viewers also had a higher fear of Islamic extremists; however, they were also more likely to fear the militia/patriot movement, white supremacists, and extreme anti-immigration groups. Those who frequently watch MSNBC had, on average, a reduced fear of Islamic extremists, extreme animal-rights groups, and the Antifa movement. Local TV news viewers were more likely to fear Islamic extremists, white supremacists, extreme environmentalists, and the Antifa movement.

What might explain the increased fears of some groups and reduced fears of others? This is due to the framing effects of particular media channels, as well as the way that particular news outlets and their followers form a shared community and rely on a common narrative vocabulary. These views create an imagined community "by employing a distinctive vocabulary that carries with it a way of seeing the community and *its adversaries*."[36] Narrowcast political media effectively create echo chambers for politicians, pundits, and media partisans. For instance, conservative outlets such as Fox News or Breitbart generate "ideologically agreeable information [that] draws conservative partisans to the protective shelter of the conservative media, where reassuring frames of argument decrease their susceptibility to other ideological points of view."[37] The increasing polarization of the electorate and the migration of viewers to media that reinforce their worldview undoubtedly apply to the devoted liberal viewers of MSNBC or the readers of Mother Jones as well.

Similar information silos and framing effects have also been demonstrated among social media users. For instance, after widespread violence and a murder at the Unite the Right rally organized by neo-Nazis in Charlottesville, Virginia, in 2017, an examination of partisan social media users found that left-wing identifiers shared headlines that identified white nationalists as the perpetrators of violence, whereas the right-wing Twittersphere took up President Trump's infamous "both sides" framing.[38]

## Islamophobia and the Media

Unfortunately, the events in Charlottesville are but one of the pernicious ways that racism and discrimination separate us into "us" and "them." There is a long history of fear of and discrimination against Muslims in the United States that can be best understood as a subdimension of racism.[39] As we will show, it must also be understood as a more specific form of xenophobia, the generalized fear of foreigners. Although Islamophobia was clearly present before the terrorist attacks of 9/11, post-9/11 media coverage increasingly framed Muslims as "others" and Islam as a violent religion.[40] In contrast to the framing of violence involving Muslim perpetrators as terrorism, the media framing of events carried out by white, domestic terrorists portrays such episodes as the acts of isolated individuals, hence posing a minimal long-term social threat.[41] This predominantly negative framing of Muslims actually did not occur immediately after 9/11, as initial coverage after the terrorist attacks in mainstream news outlets sought to differentiate most adherents of Islam from the perpetrators of terrorism. Over time, however, fringe anti-Muslim groups were able to use media frames of fear and anger that portrayed Muslims as enemies to push their views into the mainstream media.[42]

This move toward more negative media framing resulted in increasing levels of Islamophobia in the United States over time. When sociologist Penny Edgell and her colleagues first collected national data about social boundaries in the United States in 2003, they found that the most distrusted and disliked out-group among those they asked about—which included various racial and ethnic minorities, religious minorities, and gay Americans—were atheists. Muslims, although also considerably disliked at the time, came in a distant second, followed by gay men and lesbians.[43] By the time a follow-up study was conducted over a decade later, Muslims had surpassed atheists as the most distrusted and disliked out-group among the American public.[44]

This rising fear led to numerous negative outcomes for Muslim Americans. For instance, beginning in 2010, a flurry of anti-Islamic statutes were proposed at the state level that sought to ban Sharia law. By a popular vote of 70 percent, Oklahoma passed an amendment to its state constitution that year that explicitly banned Sharia law and was known as the "Save Our State Amendment."[45] Soon after passage, however, the law had an injunction placed on it and was ultimately struck down as an unconstitutional violation of the First Amendment by the 10th Circuit Court of Appeals. Because laws such as this specifically targeted a religion and were therefore unconstitutional, such provisions moved toward banning the application of international laws in American states. Such statutes were introduced in more than 30 states and passed in 8 (Arizona, Idaho, Kansas, Louisiana, North Carolina, Oklahoma, South Dakota, and Tennessee). Efforts to pass these laws were most likely to occur and be successful in conservative states with high levels of evangelical Protestant populations.[46] Although such laws are largely symbolic, they nonetheless legitimize the idea that Islam is dangerous and that Muslims are the enemies of "real" Americans. In other words, such legislative action effectively "institutionalizes fear and suspicion of Islam through bills and ballot initiatives, one state legislature at a time."[47]

The negative effects of increasing Islamophobia can also be seen in the treatment of Muslims in the United States in a variety of ways. One obvious and direct example is hate crimes. After an initial spike in anti-Muslim hate crimes in 2001, these incidents declined between 2002 and 2008. From 2009 onward, however, there was an increase in anti-Muslim hate crimes, with a severe spike in 2015 and 2016, corresponding with Donald Trump's pervasive anti-Muslim rhetoric.[48]

But poor treatment is clearly not confined only to victims of hate crimes. Other visible examples of Islamophobia can be seen in public fights over the construction of mosques in various places throughout the United States. The most famous conflict concerned plans to build an Islamic center two blocks away from the former site of the World Trade Center buildings in New York City. The so-called Ground Zero Mosque became a culture-war talking point and cable news staple in 2010. Media coverage of the controversy relied heavily on Islamophobic talking points and "experts" for arguing the case against building the Islamic center, particularly on Fox News but also in media coverage more broadly. Such coverage regularly portrayed Muslims as "explicitly menacing, irrational, and fundamentally, inherently violent."[49] Polls of the American public at the time showed that a majority opposed the building of the Islamic center, and only 20 percent supported the plan.[50]

Public controversies about the construction of mosques and Islamic community centers were not confined to New York City and flared up across America in such places as Georgia, Illinois, Tennessee, and California. Negative media framing of these events in local newspapers focused on the threat of Sharia law and terrorism, as well as the idea that Muslims are not "real" Americans.[51] Conflict over a proposed Islamic center in Murfreesboro, Tennessee, was especially acrimonious, with strong community opposition, large protests against building the mosque, and vandalism and arson on the proposed site. Local and state politicians got involved, including then–lieutenant governor Ron Ramsey, who was running in the Republican primary for governor. Asked by a constituent about the "threat invading our country from Muslims," Ramsey said he supported freedom of religion but then proceeded to further opine:

> But you cross the line when they start trying to bring Sharia Law here in the state of Tennessee, the United States. . . . Now, you could even argue whether being a Muslim is actually a religion, or is it a nationality, way of life, a cult, whatever you want to call it.[52]

The Islamic center was constructed and opened in 2012, despite multiple lawsuits intended to prevent its completion. In 2014, the Supreme Court declined to hear the case brought by opponents of the mosque, who, echoing Ramsey, argued that "Islam is not a religion, and . . . that the mosque was a threat to the community."[53]

Still another consequence of increasing Islamophobia among the public was its use by politicians, as exemplified in the fight over the Murfreesboro mosque. The reach of this political strategy went well beyond local and state politics, however, blazing a trail all the way to the White House. Donald Trump campaigned explicitly on the idea of banning all Muslims from entering the United States and followed through with a travel ban for members of majority Muslim countries once he was elected. But did such appeals really have a significant effect on vote choice in the 2016 presidential election? In short, yes. Data from a national sample of Americans taken soon after the 2016 election show that, after partisan identification, the strongest predictors of voting for Trump were a measure of Islamophobia and identifying with exclusivist visions of Christian nationalism. The strong effect of Islamophobia on the likelihood of Trump voting was robust to controls for potentially confounding issues such as sexism, antiblack prejudice, economic anxiety, and social and religious characteristics.[54] So not only did Trump's rhetoric and election incite increasing levels of Islamophobia and related hate crimes; playing on these fears was also his ticket to the top of the Republican primary field and the presidency in the first place.

Given the broad range of negative social consequences that follow from Islamophobia, we wanted to explore this dimension of fear explicitly, particularly in relation to media consumption. We asked respondents to our surveys about whether they thought Muslims should receive more screening at airports, whether Muslims were more likely to engage in terrorist activity than non-Muslims, and whether they felt comfortable with a mosque being built in their neighborhoods. Fear of terrorism was strongly related to levels of Islamophobia. And as with fear of mass shootings and terrorism, media use patterns strongly predict Islamophobia. We found an increase in Islamophobic views among viewers of Fox News, the nightly news, and local TV news. There was less fear of Muslims among national newspaper readers and MSNBC viewers.[55] The largest media consumption effects are found among regular viewers of Fox News.

That Fox News is a standout is hardly surprising. Researchers examining media consumption and politics in the United States have noted that "Fox News watchers have perceptions of political reality that differ from the rest of the television news audience."[56] In the 2018 wave of our survey, 61 percent of those who watch Fox News daily or most days said that Muslims should receive extra screening at airports, and 50 percent of those who view local television news daily or most days favored additional screening. The belief that Muslims are more likely to be terrorists than non-Muslims was shared by 59 percent of regular Fox News viewers and 40 percent of local TV watchers. Fox News and local news viewers are the *least* comfortable with mosques being built in their neighborhoods, at 57 percent and 44 percent, respectively.

In contrast, regular viewers of MSNBC were much less likely to believe Muslims engage in terrorist activities more than others (19 percent) and less likely to favor additional airport screening for Muslims (19 percent). Moreover, 78 percent of those who watch MSNBC daily said they were comfortable with having a mosque built in their neighborhoods.[57] Similarly, for daily readers of national newspapers, only 23 percent said Muslims were more likely to be terrorists, and 24 percent favored additional airport screening. More than four out of five (84 percent) daily newspaper readers said that they were comfortable having a mosque in their neighborhood. Overall, the effects of differential media framing and consumption are apparent in divergent patterns of views about Muslims.

Although Islamophobia has been on the rise since 9/11 and was capitalized on and further galvanized by Trump's campaign and governance, our surveys also show a clear backlash "Trump effect" between the 2016 and 2018 waves. Looking at the three questions that directly measured opinions about Muslims, as well as an additional policy question about whether America should cease all immigration from Muslim countries, we see Islamophobic attitudes declining across those two years among self-identified political moderates and liberals.

For the question about whether there should be additional screening for Muslim passengers in airports, support was high among conservatives (73 percent) and moderates (75 percent) in 2016 but had declined some, to 63 percent, among conservatives in 2018 and had declined considerably among moderates, down to 40 percent. Similarly, 38 percent of self-identified liberals supported additional screening in 2016, but only 12 percent supported such procedures in 2018.

There was little change across waves in the percentage of political conservatives who opposed having a mosque in their neighborhood (from 61 percent in 2016 to 57 percent in 2018). Among political moderates and liberals, there was a similar decline in opposition to a neighborhood mosque, with opposition from moderates declining from 50 percent to 33 percent and opposition from liberals declining from 22 percent to 7 percent.

Likewise, there was no change in the percentage of political conservatives who stereotyped Muslims as more likely to be terrorists between 2016 and 2018 (61 percent both years). Moderates declined some in agreement with such views, from 40 percent to 29 percent, and liberals declined substantially in this view, falling from 28 percent in 2016 to just 9 percent in 2018.

Support for Trump's travel ban policies also declined from 2016 to 2018, including slightly among self-identified conservatives, going from 47 percent to 41 percent. Notably, support was relatively low for this policy across the political spectrum, particularly in 2018. Among political moderates, 35 percent supported such a policy in 2016, but only 16 percent did in 2018. Among liberals, low levels of support got even lower over time, moving from 15 percent to 4 percent.

Overall, we see substantial declines in anti-Muslim views among the American public from 2016 to 2018, particularly among political moderates and liberals. It is worth noting that, in 2018, conservatives were the only political category where a majority expressed distrust of Muslims across the airport screening, mosque opposition, and stereotyping as terrorist questions. Fox News and its primary viewership are well in sync. At the same time, while Islamophobic and xenophobic rhetoric and policy may be an effective strategy for winning conservative primary races or safe congressional districts, such tactics will likely prove less successful in statewide races or competitive districts going forward, where winning political moderates is necessary.

So interestingly, the anti-Muslim rhetoric of the Trump administration appears to be generating the opposite effect of what was intended. Later, we document a similar effect with general xenophobia about "immigrants," showing the political and cultural interconnections between fear of foreigners, generally, and Muslims, specifically. Indeed, the overlap between fear of immigrants and Muslims is so great that inductive statistical methods designed to find underlying patterns in data cannot distinguish between measures asking about immigrants and those asking about Muslims.[58] It seems Islamophobia is not only a subset of racism in the United States; it also a subset of xenophobia. Put differently, Islamophobia in America exists at the intersection of racism and xenophobia.

## Second-Stage Effects of Terrorism and Mass Shootings

Although media coverage of terrorism and mass murder and the fear it generates are issues with important social implications, we would be remiss to not consider a critical underlying cause of the high frequency and regularity of mass murder events in the United States. For although incessant media coverage of mass killings may increase copycat events, it is clearly not the reason the United States has, by far, the most mass public shootings of any Western country. Between 1966 and 2012, the United States had 90 "rampage killers" who murdered four or more people with guns in a single episode. The next-highest country had 18 during that span. Rampage shooters in the United States were more likely to use multiple weapons and attack places of work, public spaces, and schools.[59] The most important cause of the high number and body count of such shootings in the United States is quite obvious: ease of access to guns. The United States is an international outlier on both gun ownership rates and the number of mass public shootings, and the positive relationship between these two factors holds after accounting for other issues related to mass shootings.[60] Within the American states themselves, as well as within subregions, gun ownership is positively and significantly related to increased homicide rates.[61]

Yet, even with the critical underlying issue of high firearm availability, fear has an insidious role to play. After highly publicized mass shootings in the United States, gun purchases actually *increase* due to fears about possible impending gun control legislation.[62] Furthermore, the very same people who are afraid of mass shootings and terrorism are also *more likely to be afraid of gun control*. We asked respondents to our surveys the extent to which they feared "government restrictions on firearms and ammunition." Respondents who reported being afraid of mass shootings, and especially terrorism, also feared gun control. Among those who said they were not afraid of terrorism, only 20 percent feared gun control. Among those who reported being afraid of terrorism, 51 percent reported a fear of gun control.[63] So rather than media exposure to terrifying events making the public more likely to address the root cause of such events, it actually makes the public *less* open to meaningful policy changes aimed at reducing the availability of firearms.

Horrific events of terrorism and mass murder occur with clockwork regularity in the United States. Sadly, the pervasive media coverage of such events primarily serves to heighten fear. In turn, this heightened fear leads to social withdrawal, a demonization of out-groups stereotyped as "terrorists," and a reticence about efforts to reduce gun availability. In this sense, acts of extreme violence have two stages of negative impact on society. The first stage—the death, injury, and trauma for those directly targeted in such attacks—is obvious. The second stage—the myriad negative effects of increasing fears among the public—we are only beginning to grasp. To reduce the social harm of acts of extreme violence, we must understand and address the causes of terrorism and mass murder such as firearm availability, but we must also reckon with the long-lasting aftereffects of the fear that such events generate.

# 5

## Visions of Crime

*How the Media, Satan, and Social Factors Shape Fears of Crime*

## Walking while Black

Brennan Walker, a 14-year-old from Rochester Hills, Michigan, over-slept one Thursday morning and missed his bus. Trying to walk to his high school by tracing the bus route, he became lost and began knocking on doors to ask for help. The second door he tried was the home of Jef-frey Zeigler, a 53-year-old retired firefighter. When Zeigler's wife went to the door and saw a young black man, she feared a break-in and started shouting. Zeigler charged down the stairs with his shotgun. Walker saw the gun and ran while Zeigler jumped outside and fired at the fleeing child. Luckily, Zeigler missed. Police responded to Mrs. Zeigler's call about a break-in and found Walker hiding behind a bush, crying.[1]

We like to believe we live in a world where good people would come to the aid of someone in need, not shoot at them for no reason. Simi-lar incidents to Walker's harrowing experience suggest that belief might be wrong. In nearby Dearborn Heights, Michigan, Ted Wafer shot and killed a 19-year-old black woman who knocked on his door seeking help after an auto accident.[2] In Baton Rouge, Louisiana, Japanese exchange student Yoshi Hattori was shot and killed by Rodney Peairs when Hat-tori knocked on the wrong door while heading to a Halloween party.[3] In a well-publicized case, 17-year-old Trayvon Martin, walking home after buying some candy at a store, was challenged by neighborhood watch captain George Zimmerman, who thought Martin looked "suspi-cious." In an ensuing scuffle, the watch captain shot and killed the high schooler.[4] In all four of these cases, the shooters argued that they were defending themselves. In all four cases, *no crime was occurring*. These shootings happened because of the *fear* of crime, not because of actual crime.

Fear of crime has been extensively studied by criminologists and other social scientists.[5] One key insight from this research is that the perceived likelihood of being a victim of crime and the fear of crime are related but also distinct phenomena.[6] Fear of crime is an emotional reaction affected by a broad range of personal and social factors that go far beyond the actual probability of victimization. In this chapter, we examine just how far fears about crime diverge from reality, who appears to be the most afraid of criminal victimization, and some of the negative effects that fears of crime have on society. Indeed, it is often fear of crime more than actual crime that affects our quality of life and criminal justice policy.

## Reality of Crime versus Fear of Crime

### The Reality of Crime

Americans truly are pessimistic about crime. In 2014, we asked respondents to our survey their opinion on how crime today compares to 20 years ago. For example, we asked respondents how often serial killings happen compared to two decades ago, using the possible responses of "a lot more often," "more often," "about the same amount," "less than 20 years ago," and "a lot less than 20 years ago." A little fewer than one-fifth of Americans (17 percent) said that serial killings happen *a lot more* often than 20 years ago. About another third (29 percent) think they happen more often than before. The most popular answer (43 percent) was that serial killings have not changed in their frequency in 20 years, happening just as often now as they did back in the 1990s. Only a small minority of Americans were more optimistic, thinking that serial killings have either dropped in the last 20 years (9 percent) or plummeted (2 percent).

It is easy to see why Americans are so convinced of the proliferation of serial killers. Jeffrey Dahmer, John Wayne Gacy, Ted Bundy, and others have become figures of public fascination with devoted "followings." Serial killers are the subject matter of many popular films, television crime dramas, TV newsmagazines, and countless websites. There is even a thriving market of "murderabilia" where people buy, sell, and collect objects related to serial killers, ranging from items such as artwork to body parts like hair and fingernails.[7] But Americans are wrong about the increasing prevalence of serial murder. Serial killers are in decline.

Since 1992, Mike Aamodt, a psychologist at Radford University in Virginia has been gathering data on serial killers as part of a project known as the Radford/Florida Gulf Coast University (FGCU) Serial Killer Database.[8] Combining data from court records, government agencies, websites, books, and other sources, the database provides information on the motives of serial killers, their personal characteristics (such as gender and race), and, most important for our purposes, how many were active at any given time. Since we asked our respondents in 2014 how serial killings compare to 20 years ago, let's compare 2014 to 1994. In 1994, according to Aamodt's database, there were 142 separate serial killers operating in the United States. By 2000, the number had dropped to 83. As of 2014, the number of serial killers tracked by the database was at only 25.[9]

Americans' pessimism about crime is not confined to serial killers. Since 2001, roughly two thirds of Americans have believed that the crime rate, in general, is rising.[10] But here they are wrong as well. According to the Uniform Crime Reports of the Federal Bureau of Investigation (FBI), crime is down almost 50 percent since 1993, a remarkable achievement that Americans seem to have missed.[11]

Crime statistics are complicated, to say the least. Rates can go up simply because law enforcement has cracked down on a particular crime or go down as police become more successful at catching repeat criminals. Despite such variances, one thing is clear: If you are afraid of crime, you are safer now than you used to be in most cases. Whatever you do, it would be unwise to long for the mythical "safer" days that Americans always seem to believe are behind them. At the very least, you should not long for a return to 1987, when the violent crime rate was 60 percent higher than that of 2017 and serial killers were at their highest numbers on record (172).[12]

## The Fear of Crime

Americans are entirely out of step with the trends when it comes to crime. In 2018, we asked respondents how afraid they were of 17 different

TABLE 5.1. Fear of Crime (2018) and Change in Crime-Related Fear (2015–2018).

| Crime type | Percentage of Americans who are very afraid (2018) | Change in percentage very afraid (2015–2018) |
|---|---|---|
| Random/mass shooting | 23.0 | +16.2 |
| Identity theft | 20.9 | +5.6 |
| Being hit by a drunk driver | 20.3 | +11.8 |
| Being murdered by a stranger | 15.5 | +8.8 |
| Kidnapping | 14.4 | +7.4 |
| Being sexually assaulted by a stranger | 14.4 | +7.1 |
| Police brutality | 14.0 | +6.7 |
| Racial/hate crime | 13.6 | +7.9 |
| Break-ins | 12.8 | +4.9 |
| Gang violence | 12.4 | +5.9 |
| Property theft | 12.0 | +5.2 |
| Being murdered by someone you know | 11.7 | +6.6 |
| Financial fraud (Ponzi scheme, embezzlement, etc.) | 10.9 | +3.3 |
| Mugging | 10.3 | +4.8 |
| Being sexually assaulted by someone you know | 9.5 | +3.6 |
| Stalking | 9.4 | +4.9 |

crimes, including a variety of property crimes such as theft, credit card fraud, and financial fraud, as well as a host of violent crimes, including murder, sexual assault, and mugging. Table 5.1 presents a portrait of American fear of crime, sorting crimes by the percentage of Americans who said they are "very afraid." Our survey took place in May 2018. The 12 months previous were a particularly horrifying time for mass shootings, including the school shootings in Parkland, Florida, in February 2018 and the October 2017 Harvest music festival massacre in Las Vegas. So it is not surprising that mass shootings topped our list, with nearly one fourth (23 percent) of Americans reporting high levels of fear. It is worth noting that mass shootings make up a tiny proportion of all murders. Nevertheless, the devastating consequences and unpredictability, and especially the incessant media coverage of mass shootings, have intensified fears of such events.

In a perfect world, we would have had enough time and space on our surveys to ask two questions about each type of crime, the extent to which the person fears that crime, *and* their perceived risk of being victimized by that same crime.[13] In other words, people may greatly fear being murdered by a stranger because of the seriousness of the crime and the sheer terror it would invoke, even if they know that their actual risk of such victimization is low. Conversely, people may believe that they are at high risk of being victimized by theft but have little fear of it. Previous research has found seriousness and perceived risk to be strongly related but somewhat distinct components of fear of crime.[14] Mass shootings may appear at the top of our list simply because respondents find them so terrifying, even if they do not think themselves likely to be victims. Or they may think their likelihood *has* gone up given the extensive media coverage that mass shootings have received. More than likely the high placement of mass shootings on our list is due to the fact that its horror is matched by the perception that such events are increasing.

Whether Americans are afraid because of perceived risk, perceived seriousness, or a combination of both, one thing is certain: They are becoming more afraid over time. We have been asking about the same set of crimes on our yearly surveys since 2015. Between 2015 and 2018, *fear of every crime increased.* For example, the percentage of Americans who are very afraid of financial fraud grew by 3 percentage points between 2015 and 2018. The fear of random/mass shootings increased by 16 percent in the same three-year span. So, what is driving such widespread increases in fear of crime when the crime rate is actually dropping?

To understand how fear is affected by social and personal characteristics, we conducted some in-depth analyses. We first created a fear of crime index by adding our respondents' answers about all crimes. The higher their score on this index, the more fearful they are of all types of crime. We then examined how fears of crime varied by a host of factors considered simultaneously, including gender, education, income, marital status, race/ethnicity, region of the country, residence in a metro area, political orientation, media consumption, previous criminal victimization, and various measures of religiosity.[15] Some of our findings were consistent with previous research. Others were quite surprising.

## Who Is Afraid of Crime?

### Previous Victimization

One obvious possibility when it comes to fearing crime is that being a victim previously, or knowing someone who was, would increase fear. It only makes sense. If it has happened to us before, we will fear crime happening to us again. Surprisingly, research on previous victimization and the fear of crime has shown mixed results. In those studies that found an effect of personal victimization on fear of crime, it was relatively small.[16]

In 2018, we asked our respondents if they have been the victim of a property crime or the victim of a violent crime. We also asked them if a close friend or family member has been a victim of either type of crime. After all, knowing someone who has been a victim may produce as much fear as being victimized oneself. But when we take all factors into consideration, neither previous victimization nor vicarious victimization significantly influenced fear of crime. Those who know someone who has been the victim of a property crime or violent crime are no more or less fearful of crime than those who do not know anyone who has been victimized. Even those who have been victimized by property crime or violent crime *themselves* are not more fearful of crime than are those who have been fortunate enough to avoid such victimization. Wherever our fears of crime are coming from, they are *not* from previous experience.

### Vulnerability

As discussed in Chapter 1, vulnerability plays a role in all types of fear. But speculation about the role vulnerability plays in producing fear has appeared most frequently in research on the fear of crime. In such research, personal vulnerability is often equated with physical vulnerability. Higher rates of fear among women, elderly people, and the young are attributed to a lower likelihood of being able to protect themselves during an attack.[17]

Consistent with previous research, we find that gender is a strong predictor of fear of crime, with women reporting much greater fear than men. Gender is, in fact, the strongest predictor of fear of crime out of everything we examined, by far. If we could only know a single thing about people to guess their fear of crime, their gender would be most informative. Some criminologists have argued that women's fear of sexual assault drives women's greater fear of all crime.[18] The fear of robbery, for example, may be magnified among women because a rape or sexual assault might occur during the crime. What is clear is that fear is not a direct outcome of the probability of victimization. Women are not more likely to be victims of most crimes. The most recent National Crime Victimization Survey data show that rates of overall violent victimization are not statistically different for women and men, although there is a difference in specific types of victimization.[19] Women are roughly four times more likely to suffer intimate partner violence and nearly seven times more likely to experience rape or sexual assault.[20]

Understanding fear of crime requires more than a consideration of real, or perceived, physical vulnerability. The less access people or groups have to resources that can help them cope with adverse events, the more likely they may be to fear said events, a phenomenon called social vulnerability.[21] Some characteristics that might lead to social vulnerability would include income, education, race, and age.[22] Unfortunately, achieving a higher income or getting an education will not reduce a person's level of fear about crime; neither factor has a significant effect when everything is taken into consideration. And, as we find with all types of fear, younger people are more afraid of crime.

But when it comes to social vulnerability, the strongest predictor of fear of crime is race. African American, Hispanic, and other nonwhite respondents all had significantly higher levels of fear of crime than whites. Of course, fear of crime by race is also complicated by the actual probability of victimization. As of 2015, homicide was still the leading cause of death for black men aged 15 to 34 and the second-leading cause of death for black women aged 15 to 24.[23]

## If It Bleeds, It Leads

In 2017, the Centers for Disease Control and Prevention (CDC) published a report that analyzed statistics about homicides of women in the United States from 2003 to 2014. Homicide is one of the leading causes of death for all women under the age of 44, and racial and ethnic minorities are at far greater risk.[24] When we asked women on our survey about their fear of murder, they were far more afraid of being murdered by a stranger (38 percent) than by someone they know (25 percent). Once again, the fear does not match reality. The CDC found that strangers were perpetrators in only 16 percent of all homicides in which women were the victims.[25] The majority are committed by family members, current and former partners and spouses, and friends, acquaintances, and co-workers. If a person is going to be murdered, it will most likely be by someone he or she knows.

Why is the level of fear we have about being murdered by a stranger so out of step with the actual risk? In a fascinating study conducted by scholars at the school of public health at the University of California, Susan Sorensen and her colleagues gathered detailed data on the 9,442 homicides committed in Los Angeles County, California, between 1990 and 1994.[26] They examined how these homicides were covered by the largest newspaper in the area, the *Los Angeles Times*. An obvious, but important fact, is immediately apparent; not all homicides are reported in the news. The *Los Angeles Times* produced 2,782 stories about homicides between 1990 and 1994, a fraction of the actual number. Some deaths are deemed more newsworthy than others.

The most common type of homicide occurred in the street between two people who knew one another. Most involved a single victim, and the perpetrator was of the same race as the victim. The majority of victims were men (85 percent), nonwhite (85 percent), and between the ages of 15 and 34 (68 percent). Such homicides rarely made the papers. The deaths of young men of color were tragically not deemed newsworthy.

In contrast to the realities of homicide, news stories were most likely to cover homicides where the victims were women, white or Asian, and younger than 15 or older than 65.[27] The likelihood of coverage increased to the extent that the case involved multiple victims, a killing that occurred inside the home, when perpetrators were strangers to the victims, and when the victim was white and the killer a minority. Victims who had an income of $35,000 or above were more than twice as likely to have their murders appear in the newspaper than were people slain who were poor. If you are an older white woman with a higher level of income, we can virtually guarantee that you will not be murdered by a stranger in your home. But we can definitely guarantee that in the extremely rare event that it did happen, it will make the news—for weeks on end. When it comes to media coverage of crime, the amount of coverage follows what we call the *law of inverse proportionality*. As an aphorism, media coverage is inversely related to a crime's actual likelihood.

That the news covers rare events is only natural. Media outlets cannot sell newspapers and ad space or gather views unless they attract our attention. Per humans' responses to fear, our eyes are not drawn to the commonplace. The problem occurs when we assume, almost always erroneously, that the fact that we have seen a crime in the news means it is common or becoming more common. The news media definitely exacerbates this effect. Should a crime involve what is considered an extremely innocent or vulnerable person, a seemingly "new" form of crime, and/or a particularly strange or horrific form of predation, it will attract significant media attention. The "success" engendered by such a news story encourages the media to be on the lookout for, or even actively search for, other, similar crimes. What at first seemed a singular act has suddenly blown up into an alarming "trend" or a "crime wave." Finding crimes that were previously being ignored does not mean they are happening more often. In fact, if the media can find five similar horrific crimes, we might choose to be comforted that is all they found, despite a concerted effort. This phenomenon, whereby rare crimes become trends via media attention, is so well known to deviance researchers and criminologists that they have given it a fancy name: "deviancy amplification spiral."[28]

In 2012, a crime that ticked all the requisite boxes necessary for the invention of a new "crime wave" occurred in Miami Beach, Florida. On May 26, Rudy Eugene, the 31-year-old son of Haitian immigrants, brutally attacked an older homeless man. Eugene had already ripped off his clothes when he encountered Ronald Poppo and began assaulting him. A passing bicyclist came across a horrific scene, finding Eugene biting Poppo on the face. He alerted police. The responding officer, Jose Ramirez, warned Eugene to stop but received only growls in return. Ramirez ultimately fired five shots at Eugene, killing him. The crazed Eugene had bitten off most of Poppo's face, leaving him horrifically scarred and severely disabled for life. The extraordinary violence and senselessness of the attack led police to speculate that Eugene was under the influence of "bath salts," a relatively new form of a synthetic designer drug, the complete effects of which were still unclear. Media outlets covered the incident extensively and some began to argue that bath salts-related crimes were a major new trend. By June 1, 2012, ABC News had dredged up enough cases of people committing crimes while on bath salts to propose that the "Face-Eating Cannibal Attack May Be Latest in String of 'Bath Salts' Incidents."[29] Unfortunately, the shelf life of the Eugene case as an exemplar for a new wave of bath salts crimes was cut short when toxicology tests determined that he did not even have the drug in his system. To their credit, many media outlets reported Eugene's toxicology results. But corrections to previous stories rarely receive as much attention as the original, attention-grabbing claims. Stories about "bath salts zombies" still appear in the news.[30]

The media clearly plays a central role in creating a fear of crime that does not match reality. Media is the lens through which perceptions of crime are refracted from reality. To explore the extent to which the consumption of media shapes fears about crime, we included in our analysis a host of questions about respondents' media-related habits. Using a scale ranging from "never" to "every day," we asked how often respondents read a local newspaper or a national newspaper such as *USA Today* or the *New York Times*.[31] We asked about how often people watched various news sources, including local TV news, the national network news, and specific networks such as MSNBC, Fox News, and CNN, as well as daytime talk shows such as *The View*. Finally, we asked how often respondents got their news from websites, talk radio shows, and social media sources. The breadth of our fear of crime and news consumption measures allows us to conduct one of the deepest explorations of the relationship between media consumption and fear of crime to date.[32] Several patterns were immediately clear.

First, as other scholars have found, watching local TV news is associated with higher levels of fear of crime.[33] Those who watch their local TV news every day exhibit a fear of all types of crime that is 26 percent higher than those who never watch. Local TV news had a similar effect when only considering fear of violent crimes. Those who watch their local TV news every day are 24 percent more fearful of violent crime than those who never do. The effect of local TV news is especially pronounced when we consider only property crimes. Those who never watch their local TV news are 30 percent less fearful of property crimes than are those who watch every day. Clearly, hearing about crimes that are occurring in your local community is associated with heightened fear. And you will assuredly hear about local crimes often. Previous research has demonstrated that crime is the second-most frequently covered topic on local broadcasts, following the traffic and weather.[34] Only stories about one of these three things are likely to stick in your memory for very long. Also airing on local channels are a variety of daytime television shows, and the more frequently people watch such shows, the higher their fear of crime.

Fear of crime is also higher among people who watch fictionalized crime drama shows, such as *CSI* and *Law & Order*, but primarily for those who report watching such shows very frequently.[35] There is a stronger relationship between fear of crime and viewing "true crime" TV shows, such as *Dateline* and *America's Most Wanted*. Any amount of viewing true-crime shows was related to increased fear of crime. About one fourth (26 percent) of people who never watched true-crime shows scored above the sample mean on fear of crime, compared to more than half of those (56 percent) who watched such programs daily.

Interestingly, fear of crime is also associated with watching all kinds of partisan news. If you watch Fox News every day, then you are going to be significantly more afraid of crime than those who never watch. On average, a person who watches Fox News every day is 30 percent more fearful of crime than someone who completely avoids the network. But whatever is happening here is not simply a consequence of how a right-leaning network covers crime. Those who report watching MSNBC with greater frequency are *also* more afraid of crime than are those who watch less. Everyday watchers of MSNBC are 18 percent more afraid of all types of crime than are those who never watch. We thought perhaps viewers of each partisan network would be afraid of different crimes, but this was not the case. Looking at patterns of fear for each of the specific crimes we asked about, viewing partisan news was associated with across the board increases in fear of all types of crime. The effects of Fox News were slightly stronger and were more pronounced with regard to fear of terrorism, but otherwise, the general trend was that more partisan news viewing equated with a greater fear of all types of crime.

At present, little research on fear of crime and the possible effects of consuming Internet news sources has been conducted.[36] What research has been done finds no relationship between getting one's news from websites and fearing crime.[37] Neither do we. But no previous work has examined whether getting one's news from *social media* (such as Twitter, Facebook, etc.) is associated with fear of crime. Indeed, it is and strongly so. People who get their news from social media have levels of fear, on average, 26 percent higher than people who never do. The way people receive their news and entertainment is changing rapidly in the digital age, and the full consequences of these changes remain uncertain. But it seems that increased use of social media will also increase public fears about criminal victimization. The fact that media usage has such a profound impact on fear of crime, while actual victimization does not, tells us how important *perceptions* of danger and crime frequency, as opposed to actual risk or experience, are in determining our fears.

### On Good and Evil

When crimes occur, particularly the most heinous and violent, media portrayal of the criminal as "evil" is common.[38] Parsing the confluence of upbringing, psychological issues, frustrations, availability of weapons, access to vulnerable targets, and other factors that influence the decision to victimize others is complicated. Evil is a shortcut for describing and simplifying horrible crimes.

If we tend to view crime as evil, particularly those crimes that frighten us the most, then religious beliefs that tell people about the nature of existential good and evil should influence beliefs about crime.[39] Conservative religious theology has long played a fundamental role in shaping American politics and is a well-established predictor of a variety of political and moral attitudes.[40] Different religious beliefs or practices might specifically influence our fear of crime in different ways. If people actively engage with a religious community and strongly believe in a powerful God, they might be less afraid of crime, as that God could protect them. There are often sacred scriptures speaking to this, such as Hebrews 13:6 in the Christian Bible: "So that we may boldly say, The Lord is my helper, and I will not fear what man shall do unto me."[41] Conversely, however, if we believe in a powerful supernatural force of evil, such as Satan, we may believe that he will actively try to harm us in a variety of ways. Or believing in supernatural evil may simply lead us to see criminals as truly evil themselves, increasing our fear of them.

Despite the extensive literature in criminology and sociology on the predictors and consequences of fear of crime, the effect that religion and religious beliefs may have on the fear of crime has remained virtually unexplored. We found only one study that focused on trying to examine the influence of religiosity and religious beliefs on fears about crime. It reported a moderate negative relationship between frequency of religious participation and fear of property crime in a small sample of people living in the western part of the state of Georgia.[42] Aside from this, social scientists have not explored the possible relationship between religion and fear of crime at all. Even researchers studying fear of crime using data sets explicitly designed to measure religion omit this factor.[43] Other scholars using data taken from a religious sample noted that preliminary analyses of the relationship between religiosity and fear of crime "indicate that religiosity is not a significant predictor."[44] Given that a wide range of different dimensions of religiosity are known to be strong predictors of views about how criminals should be punished, it would be surprising if religious views did not predict levels of crime-related fear in some way.[45]

To bring a new approach to the question of how religion relates to fear of crime, we included multiple indicators of religiosity in our analyses. We asked respondents how often they attended religious services, whether they thought the Bible is the literal word of God, and the type of religious group with which they affiliate, if any.[46] To determine whether the belief in evil forces would increase fear of crime, we asked respondents two additional questions about whether they believe the devil and demons exist, using the possible responses of "definitely does not exist," "probably does not exist," "probably exists," and "definitely exists."

Studies that have examined patterns of beliefs about religious evil have found high levels of belief in Satan and his minions in the United States.[47] Our study is no different. More than 40 percent of Americans (42 percent) are entirely certain that the devil exists, with another fifth (21 percent) thinking he probably does. Similar numbers believe in demons. More than half of Americans say that demons definitely (36 percent) or probably (24 percent) exist. A third of Americans are certain of the existence of both the devil and his army of evil underlings. We created a belief in evil measure by adding these two items together. The higher a respondent's score, the more he or she believes in supernatural forces of evil. We included this in our analyses predicting fear of crime, along with the other measures of religiosity.

Our analyses show that religion can have both beneficial and negative effects when it comes to fear of crime. Importantly, what kind of religion a person belongs to did not matter. Protestants were no more or less frightened of crime than Catholics. Jews were just as afraid of crime as agnostics, or those with no religious or secular identification at all. But no matter what kind of religion people claim, attending communal services *does* have an impact on their level of fear. Those who went to church, temple, or mosque most often had the lowest levels of fear about crime. Communal participation makes us less fearful of our fellow humans. In a similar vein, the cognitive certainty of believing that the Bible is the literal word of God seems to have a protective effect when it comes to fear of crime. Those who believed in a literal Bible were significantly less afraid of crime than were those who did not, controlling for other factors.[48]

But larger than these religion effects is the influence of beliefs about supernatural evil. Someone who believes in the devil and demons tends to exhibit much higher levels of fear about crime than someone who does not. The effect of evil is quite pronounced. A person who scores the maximum on the beliefs in supernatural evil measure (absolute belief in the devil and demons) has, on average, a 22 percent higher level of crime-related fear than does someone who has the minimum score (complete disbelief in both). Belief in Satan and demons was the second-strongest predictor in our models. As noted earlier, if we wanted to guess how much you fear crime and could only know one thing about you, it would be gender. If you allowed us to gather two pieces of information, we will kindly ask for your thoughts about the devil and demonic activity. Going forward, research on fear of crime should consider and account for beliefs about evil and further specify how views about the "transgressive" supernatural influence people's fears about crime and criminals.

### Fear Hunters

FBI profilers have become legendary figures within law enforcement and entertainment for their ability to provide psychological and behavioral

TABLE 5.2. A Profile of Fearing Crime (2018).

| Characteristic | Influence on fear of crime |
| --- | --- |
| Woman | Increased fear |
| Belief in the devil and demons | Increased fear |
| Religious service attendance | Decreased fear |
| Hispanic | Increased fear |
| Other race (not white, black, or Hispanic) | Increased fear |
| Younger | Increased fear |
| Watching daytime television | Increased fear |
| Black | Increased fear |
| Watch local TV News | Increased fear |
| Watch MSNBC | Increased fear |
| Watch Fox News | Increased fear |
| Biblical literalist | Decreased fear |
| Get news from social media | Increased fear |
| Conservative politically | Increased fear |

Characteristics that had no effect, controlling for other factors: education, income, marital status, region of the country, metro/rural status, religious tradition, other forms of media usage (national newspaper, network news, CNN, talk radio, online news), and previous victimization (property and/or violent) of oneself or a friend or family member.

portraits of serial killers, bombers, and other criminals. The image of an FBI "mind hunter" who must match wits with a fiendishly clever serial killer has become a common entertainment trope.[49] We can provide a similar "profile," not of a criminal but of those that *fear* criminals. Table 5.2 presents all the personal characteristics that we found to be significantly related to fearing crime. We have ordered these characteristics by the size of their effects. As discussed previously, the strongest predictor of one's fear of crime is gender, followed by belief in the devil and demons. With the exception of religious service attendance and being a biblical literalist, the more of these characteristics you hold, the higher we expect your fear of crime to be.

Among the myriad of personal, religious, and media usage characteristics that form our "fear profile," one thing is conspicuously absent: actual experience with crime. Knowing that people have been previously victimized by violent or property crime tells us nothing about their potential level of fear, nor does the previous victimization of their friends and family. All these victimization factors have no effect on fear of crime. What all this tells us is that fear of crime is about the things people *believe* about crime (and the sources of these beliefs, whether religious or media-based) than the reality of crime. Americans think that crime is increasing when it is not and correspondingly develop fears about crime that are disconnected from experience.

Why does this matter? Should we care if people are more afraid of crime than they should be?

## Consequences of Fearing Crime

### Fear and Punishment

Unfortunately, the fears that we develop about crime, whether they are tied to reality or not, have real effects on our beliefs and behaviors.[50] These changes in outlook and actions ultimately affect our communities and the wider society. Our fears of crime restrict our movements and willingness to use public spaces such as parks.[51] The tendency of news coverage about crime to focus on those committed by minorities increases racial tensions.[52] Fear of crime plays a role in the flight of higher-income families from our central cities.[53]

One consequence of fearing crime with particularly pernicious effects is its relationship with harsh punitive attitudes toward criminals. The American public is surprisingly punitive, particularly given our decreasing crime rates and already extremely high incarceration rate. In fact, these high levels of punitiveness are a primary cause of the harsh penal policies that have created mass incarceration in the United States.[54]

In 2014, we asked respondents to our survey how they think criminals should be treated. The basic question asked if "the criminal justice system should . . ." and then had specific items for "make sentences more severe for all crimes," "use the death penalty for juveniles who murder," "limit the appeals available for death sentences," "use 'three strikes' laws for repeat offenders," "use chemical castration on sex offenders," and "reduce the privileges available to prisoners (televisions, recreation, etc.)."[55] Each question had answer choices ranging from "strongly disagree" to "strongly agree." By adding the responses to these questions, we created a composite measure of punitiveness toward criminals. The higher a person's score, the more harshly they wanted criminals to be treated.

We used respondents' fear of crime to predict punitive attitudes toward criminals while also controlling for demographic characteristics, frequency of watching TV, religious characteristics, and political leanings. Key factors that led individuals to be less punitive in their orientation were higher levels of education, being African American, and frequently attending religious services. The three factors that have the largest effect on making people *more* punitive are being politically conservative, believing in Satan, and fearing crime, in that order.

The fact that race plays a large role in punitive attitudes once again highlights the importance of fear versus reality. Black respondents in our survey were twice as likely to have been victims of a violent crime (30 percent) than whites (15 percent) and far more likely (68 percent vs. 40 percent) to have a close friend or family member who has been violently victimized.[56] Accordingly, African Americans are more fearful of crime. The average African American respondent to our survey had a fear of crime 28 percent higher than the average white respondent. But even if they *do* fear crime, African Americans do not let that fear translate into punitiveness. When we separate our respondents by racial groups, fear of crime has no effect on punitive attitudes among African Americans. Put another way, African Americans who were extremely afraid of crime were not harsher toward criminals than those who were not afraid of crime at all.

In contrast, punitiveness among white respondents increases steadily and significantly with fear of crime.[57] Furthermore, this relationship between fear of crime and punitiveness among white Americans is completely mediated by another fear: xenophobia.[58] In other words, fear of crime increases punitiveness by increasing white Americans' fears about foreigners and immigrants—those who are socially "other" compared to whites. Put simply, white people have less to fear from crime than do black people, but when white people are afraid, they are far more likely to want to punish those they label as rule breakers. In this sense, a general fear of crime is not driving harsh views of criminals and support for the policies of mass incarceration, but rather, *white fear* is.

## The Functions and Dysfunctions of Crime-Related Fear

One of the most debilitating effects that the fear of crime could potentially have on our social fabric is in isolating us from one another. Previous research has found that fear about crime is associated with heightened perceptions of danger in neighborhoods and reduced satisfaction with one's neighborhood and community.[59] Insecurity and fear for one's safety can, in turn, lead individuals to withdraw from their communities by spending more time at home and less time getting to know their neighbors.[60] Once fear has led us to withdraw, we also become less likely to donate to and volunteer with community organizations.[61] Ironically, the things that fears lead us to do (or not do) can become self-fulfilling prophecies. When we retreat from our neighborhoods, we experience weaker community organizations, more signs of disorder (such as vandalism and graffiti), deteriorating business conditions, and neighborhood flight as residents seek "safer" environments.[62] All these consequences of retreat are associated with higher crime rates.[63] When we fear crime, we ironically make more of it.

All this previous research suggests that fear of crime should have a simple relationship with engaging with your community; the more you are afraid, the less you will involve yourself. What we found was more complicated and one of the great surprises of our research.

Our 2015 survey included a series of questions that tap the extent to which respondents were involved in their communities. We asked respondents about nine different ways they could be engaged with their neighbors, including how often they have attended an event at a public place, attended any public meeting that included a discussion of local or school affairs, attended a club or organizational meeting, had friends come to their home, socialized with co-workers outside of work, been in the home of someone who lives in a different neighborhood (or had them to their home), met personally with someone considered a community leader, donated blood, or volunteered. We added these items together to create a "civic engagement" index. The higher respondents' scores, the more involved they were with helping their communities.[64]

We then predicted the likelihood that our respondents would engage with their community based on their demographics, previous victimization, fear of crime, and other factors.[65] What we found was a relationship

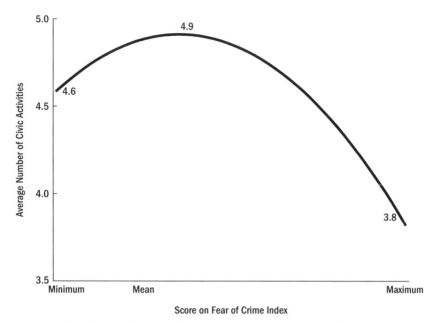

Figure 5.1. Curvilinear Relationship between Fear of Crime and Number of Civic Engagement Activities in the Past Year (2015).

between fear of crime and community involvement that was not simple and straightforward. Civic engagement did not simply decrease steadily as fear of crime increased. Rather, what we found was a curvilinear effect (see Figure 5.1).

Again, a curvilinear effect is one in which the highest or lowest values of the outcome are at the mid-values of the predictor.[66] In this case, the highest levels of civic engagement occur at mid-levels of fear of crime. Figure 5.1 displays how levels of civic engagement varied by levels of fear about crime. While civic engagement is relatively high among those who do not fear crime at all, levels of engagement actually increase initially as fear of crime increases. The highest average levels of civic engagement occur among those who are just above the sample mean in their fear of crime. But then things reach a tipping point. As the fear of crime reaches its highest levels, community engagement begins to decline precipitously as, apparently, people retreat into greater isolation. By far, the lowest levels of civic engagement are among those with the most fear about crime. This finding suggests that, at moderate levels, fearing crime may modestly *help* communities by spurring greater levels of engagement but can become dysfunctional when it reaches higher levels. Why would this happen?

Although most research on how crime-related fear impacts communities has assumed fear of crime to be entirely dysfunctional or harmful, a few dissenting voices have been calling for a more nuanced understanding of the relationship. In a seminal article written in 1981, criminologist James Garofalo chastised other researchers for assuming the fear of crime is an "unmitigated evil that must be eliminated completely."[67] When people fear crime, he argued, they may take the sensible precautions necessary to avoid being victimized.[68] Furthermore, that individuals who fear crime might take action to try to prevent it in their neighborhoods is reasonable. This may simply take the form of purchasing a home alarm, but fear might also lead to a person to join or form a community group designed to watch for and deter crime or to increase communication with neighbors to share information about crime.[69] In Garofalo's view, the "complete absence of fear" would be problematic.[70]

Garofalo did not, however, think that unfettered fear of crime would be helpful. Moderate fear might motivate us, but high levels of fear will harm us:

> Increases in the intensity of fear quickly become dysfunctional . . . because responses, both behavioral and attitudinal, go beyond what is necessary to prevent victimization and produce effects such as unnecessary avoidance of potentially rewarding social interactions and unwarranted distrust of others.[71]

Following this line of reasoning, British criminologists Jonathan Jackson and Emily Gray separate the fear of crime into *functional* and *dysfunctional* components. A functional fear of crime acts as a motivator, inspiring greater precautionary measures or engagement with prevention programs that might curb crime.[72] A dysfunctional fear of crime is characterized by excessive worry, which can result in pessimism, retreat, and avoidance.[73] Our finding suggests that, indeed, fear of crime can actually be functional at low and moderate levels until it reaches excessive levels. When residents of a neighborhood begin to fear crime due to a perceived increase in physical signs of disorder or a perceived increase in criminal activity, this increased fear and aware-ness may motivate them to build ties with neighbors and participate in neighborhood groups as a means of protecting their investment in that neighborhood.[74] But when fear of crime reaches a "tipping point," individuals retreat from their neighborhoods, minimize their perceived risk by avoiding public places, limit contact with others in the neighbor-hood, and perhaps even entirely divest from the neighborhood, seeking a new one, at least if they are able.[75]

## Self-Victimization

Addressing Americans' fear of crime is complicated. Fear of crime is rising at the same time actual crime is dropping. People long for a safer time that does not really exist. Those who are least likely to be victimized are the most fearful of crime. People who have never been criminally victimized are often far more punitive toward criminals than are those who have. The media shows us the rarest and most gruesome crimes, leaving us with the impression that they are common. Not surprisingly, such stories make deep impressions in our memories.

It seems modern societies will forever have to grapple with fear about crime that is built on fantastical notions. Further reductions in the crime rate will not have much effect on fear if a 50 percent decline has not already.[76] Nor can we expect the media to stop covering rare and vio-lent crime or to start producing headlines about all-too-common crimes such as domestic violence. News outlets need ratings and profits, and people are more likely to pay attention to shocking information.[77]

To conclude, however, that the fear of crime is entirely harmful would be a mistake. Crime may be on the decline, but that does not mitigate the horror experienced by those who are the victims of violence. A singular focus on the discrepancy between fear and actual crime rates could belittle the experience of victims. Fear can also be functional, as a small amount leads us to provide greater resources for victims, de-velop educational programs about minimizing risk, and encourage citi-zens to take sensible precautions and engage with their neighbors in crime prevention programs. But the greater our level of fear, it seems, the more harmful the gap between fantasy and reality becomes. If we believe that evildoers hide behind every corner and we see malice in the face of every stranger, we will retreat rather than engage. If we allow our strongly held myths about crime, such as "stranger danger" and the belief that we are most likely to be victimized by people of other races to take root, we will focus attention in the wrong place. We may even come to see a child at our door looking for help as an imminent threat. We should all fear such a world.

# 6

## Consequences of Fear

We have detailed different aspects of the many fears that Americans hold, as well as the sources and patterns of these fears. But, to be frank, so what if someone believes in an assortment of conspiracy theories or has an intense fear of immigrants? What difference does it make if someone is afraid of crime or terrorism, even if that fear is not in step with the actual risk of victimization? The time has come to look more closely at some of the consequences of fear for both individuals who are fearful and society more broadly. Although highly personal, fear is not an isolated emotion. Rather, it is a state of mind that is intimately connected to a wide range of psychological, sociological, and political outcomes. Although we clearly cannot map all the myriad consequences of fear, we can highlight some of the important ways fear shapes people's lives and communities. Put simply, there are many reasons to fear . . . fear.

### Consequences of Conspiracism

Seven out of 10 Americans believe in something that could be considered a "conspiracy theory," and these beliefs are strongly related to personal levels of fear.[1] But does believing in a world of conspiratorial plots and schemes also influence people's well-being or their communities? Although specific individuals are undoubtedly idiosyncratic in their fear profiles, our surveys offer an opportunity to look at broad patterns in how conspiracism relates to a range of psychological and social outcomes. To look at how believing in conspiracy theories relates to psychological well-being, we examined levels of anxiety and paranoia across different levels of conspiracism. The anxiety metric combined responses for how often respondents reported that, during the past two weeks, they felt restless, easily annoyed, afraid something terrible would happen, that they could not trust anyone, that people were taking advantage of them, and that they were being watched or talked about by others. As expected, there is a significant positive relationship between reported levels of anxiety and the average number of conspiracies respondents believed. This pattern is primarily concentrated among people who reported high levels of anxiety (meaning more than one standard deviation above the sample mean on the anxiety measure). Americans with high levels of anxiety believed in an average of five conspiracies. Those reporting no anxiety averaged the lowest number of conspiracies believed. In short, people who believe in a lot of conspiracy theories also tend to have higher levels of anxiety and paranoia. The relationship between conspiratorial beliefs and anxiety and paranoia is reciprocal and mutually reinforcing. The "paranoid style" of conspiracism has not only psychological roots but also psychological consequences.[2]

In addition to psychological consequences, there are social consequences of conspiratorial thinking. One particularly important social consequence of conspiracism is decreased trust, which is a critical component of a civic and democratic society, the proverbial glue that holds together positive, cooperative social interactions.[3] Conspiracy belief was the strongest predictor of distrust of other people. The more conspiracies people accept, the lower their average level of trust. Among those who did not believe in any of the conspiracies, most (75 percent) reported that at no point in the past two weeks had they "felt that it is not safe to trust anyone." Only about half of those who believed in four or more conspiracies felt safe trusting others in the past two weeks. Among hyper-conspiracists—those who believed all the different conspiracy theories—60 percent did not feel safe trusting other people the past two weeks. In many ways, conspiracy theories are ideological responses to distrust. Tragically, conspiracies only deepen that initial distrust, spurring even greater reticence to trust others, and increased levels of perceived threat.

There are also specific and direct political consequences of conspiracism.[4] Consider the ever-present political debate and social conflict in the United States over gun control. In a multivariate model controlling for all the relevant variables related to levels of conspiracism or gun control attitudes—including demographics, political identity, religion, trust in others, anxiety and paranoia, overall phobias, xenophobia, and Islamophobia—the strongest predictor of whether Americans fear gun control is their acceptance of conspiracy theories.[5] At the minimum of the conspiracism index, the probability of fearing gun control was relatively low (.11). At the mean level of conspiracism, the predicted probability was .35, and at the highest level of conspiracism, the probability of fearing gun control was very high (.77). This connection explains the regularity of conspiracy theories circulating immediately after, and then persisting long after, mass public shootings. Not only are those who believe strongly in conspiracies more likely to fear gun control; they are also much more likely than other Americans to report that they have purchased a gun out of fear. Those who scored at the highest levels of conspiratorial belief were more than four times as likely as those who disbelieved in all the conspiracies to report buying a gun out of fear.[6]

This, too, is a vicious cycle. As conspiracy theories proliferate in the digital age—a communication environment uniquely amenable to the spread of such ideas—gun control will become even more difficult in the United States.[7]

## It's a Mean, Mean World

To the extent that digital technology helps with the spread of conspiracy theories, we can expect public distrust to rise. But we may face an even more fundamental problem. Some scholars believe that media usage, in general, even if it is not about conspiracies, can lead to the belief that other people cannot be trusted. Part of this connection is, no doubt, due to the media's tendency to focus on the attention-grabbing, rare, and unusual, thereby distorting our understanding of the frequency of disturbing events. In 1976, communications scholars George Gerbner and Larry Gross proposed an even more straightforward connection.[8] They argued that the frequency with which we see images and messages in our entertainment increases the likelihood that we will believe those images reflect an underlying reality. The more one views television, they claimed, the more violent images one will see. Viewing of these violent images will, in turn, cultivate a general sense in the viewer that the world is a dangerous place and that other people cannot be trusted.[9] Gerbner and colleagues later coined the term *mean world syndrome* to describe this phenomenon.[10] Given the time when their work was conducted,

Gerbner and Gross focused on television, but subsequent research has called for examining the role of new media forms in cultivating views of a dangerous world.[11]

An insidious effect of developing a view of others as untrustworthy and evil is that it may make us less likely to help others when they need it. We may even become less likely to *accept* help when we need it. If our fears about the world keep us from helping others in need, we will inadvertently create the mean world we believe in.

In 2016 our survey asked respondents two important questions about a situation anyone could face: running out of gas on the highway or coming across someone else who has. Using answers ranging from "strongly disagree" to "strongly agree," respondents told us if they would "feel safe giving them help" if a stranger ran out of gas, as well as whether they would feel safe "asking a stranger for help" if they ran out of gas. We created models to predict one's likelihood of giving or receiving help. A key reason that a person might not help others or accept help is the fear that those others will victimize him or her in some way. Such fears are fostered by the occasional news stories that discuss a case where a "Good Samaritan" was attacked. For example, in May 2018, a man who crashed his car near Cleveland attacked several people who tried to help him.[12] Of course, we will never know of all the cases where people helped one another by the road without incident, as such acts of kindness are, sadly, hardly newsworthy. Knowing already that media usage is associated with increased fear of crime, we included respondents' levels of crime-related fear in our models. We also included measures of media consumption, previous criminal victimization, key demographics, and religiosity.

For the willingness to receive help from a stranger, gender and fear of crime dwarfed all others in our analysis. Men are far more willing to receive help from strangers, but to the extent that they fear crime, the likelihood goes down dramatically.[13] Furthermore, some types of media consumption are directly creating images of a mean world over and above any effects they have on the general fear of crime. Those who report watching local news show less willingness to accept help from strangers. The characteristics of those who are more willing to offer help to strangers are quite similar to those willing to accept it. Men and those with lower levels of fear of crime are the most likely to help by a wide margin.[14] Unfortunately, people with higher levels of education are less likely to stop and help, as are those uncertain about God's existence and people who watch local news. For both receiving and giving help, we were surprised to find a moderate but significant *positive* effect of being the previous victim of property crime and a willingness to give and receive help. This reinforces that *perceptions* about crime are far more important than the realities of crime, even for those who have been victimized in the past.

The ultimate lesson here is that certain forms of media do, indeed, dampen our willingness to help and receive help from others, especially local news, which often prominently features stories about crime. The more information we get from such media, the less likely we are to help one another. Actual incidents of criminal victimization on the side of the road during situations where motorists attempt to help one another are extremely rare. We must ask ourselves: If all of us who have good intentions let fear keep us from helping others, who will be left to help those who need it? Who will be left to help us? A scary prospect.

## Fearing the "Other": Consequences of Xenophobia

Another manifestation of fear with pernicious psychological and social consequences is xenophobia, the fear of foreigners and immigrants. Xenophobia manifests as a general sense of what sociologists call "minority threat," where powerful groups fear, and thereby seek to control and punish, minority groups.[15] Although xenophobia is related to racism, these issues must be also be distinguished.[16] People may be xenophobic without being (at least overtly) racist toward specific people groups, and larger shares of populations will publicly admit to having disdain toward "immigrants" compared to those voicing antipathy toward specific groups. At the same time, nearly all those who are racist toward specific groups will also be xenophobic toward "foreigners." In other words, "racists will also tend to be xenophobes, but less likely the inverse."[17]

Psychologists have found that human infants are hardwired to categorize others through firsthand cognitive processes. For instance, infants ranging from 9 to 14 months old consistently display preferences for those who share similar physical characteristics over those who do not.

Furthermore, infants are more likely to favor those who punish others who are dissimilar.[18] Clearly, babies are not able to use moral reasoning in such assessments, providing evidence that out-group biases, as well as the categorization of "us" and "them," are deeply ingrained in humans' innate cognitive processes.[19] The fear of people who are in some way markedly different is an inherited predisposition in humans and one that we must consciously work to overcome.

In its most extreme forms, xenophobia can manifest as moral panics, ritual executions, and genocide.[20] In addition to violent collective responses to xenophobia, socially isolated individuals may also lash out by violently acting on apocalyptic visions of xenophobia. In a horrific example of how xenophobia can lead to violence, especially when combined with conspiracism, on October 27, 2018, a lone gunman entered a Jewish temple in Pittsburgh and killed 11 worshippers, most of them elderly. The killer left a trail of not only anti-Semitic but also virulently xenophobic material online, espousing conspiracy theories about "invaders" that "kill our people" and "white genocide" at the hands of immigrants and Jews.[21] In cases such as this mass murder at a synagogue, xenophobia becomes both motivation and justification for the cold-blooded murder of innocent people.

But even more mundane forms of xenophobia also have serious negative social consequences and are far more widespread. Like conspiracism, fear of immigrants is highly correlated with fear of gun control and purchasing a gun out of fear. But this tendency is even stronger among Americans with high levels of xenophobia than it is among those with high levels of conspiracism. Xenophobia is the strongest predictor of fearing gun control, outpacing both political identity and conspiracism. Xenophobia is also the strongest predictor of whether someone reported purchasing a gun out of fear. Among Americans with the lowest levels of xenophobia, the probability of purchasing a gun in response to fear is low (.08). At the highest levels of xenophobia, it is more than five times as high (.42).

As we have seen, a primary consequence of fear is that it undermines social trust. This is especially the case with xenophobia. When given a forced-choice question about whether most people can be trusted, those who were afraid of foreigners were far less likely to report general social trust. Among those in the lowest quartile of scores on the xenophobia index, only 26 percent said "you can't be too careful in life" rather than saying they generally trusted most people or that "it all depends." In contrast, among those with scores on the xenophobia measure in the highest quartile, more than twice are many (58 percent) selected "you can't be too careful in life." This reveals yet another negative consequence of fearing outsiders. The accompanying heightened threat detection and vigilance undermine an individual's ability to trust their neighbors.

Fear of outsiders also proved consequential to explaining something that initially baffled pundits, scholars, and the public alike: the unprecedented political rise of Donald Trump. When Trump sailed down an escalator and announced his bid for the presidency with a rambling speech at Trump Tower in Manhattan, mainstream media and commentators were aghast by his broad characterization of Mexican immigrants as "bringing crime" and drugs but most especially by his comment that "they're rapists." Similarly, his call to ban all Muslims from traveling to the United States was initially met with derision by those who noted the proposed policy's obvious violation of First Amendment rights to freedom of religion. Many wrote off such demagoguery as having no place in American politics, but Trump's denigration of outsiders proved to be his ticket to the top of a crowded Republican primary field. Likewise, Islamophobia, coupled with shoring up the evangelical Protestant base of the Republican Party through appeals to exclusivist Christian nationalism, proved to be the most important predictors of who ultimately voted for Trump in the 2016 election.[22]

Trump's hardline stance against immigrants continued after his election, with controversial policies such as a rebranded (Muslim) "travel ban" and the separation of migrant children from their parents at the southern border between the United States and Mexico. Not surprisingly, scores on the xenophobia index are strongly tethered to support for Trump's travel ban and border wall policies to the extent that measures of views about those policies actually load on the xenophobia index in factor analyses, meaning that, statistically speaking, *these policies are a direct extension of xenophobic ideas*.[23] Not coincidentally, famed Watergate and presidential journalist Bob Woodward's book about the inner workings of the Trump administration was titled *Fear*.[24]

Trump's punitive rhetoric also continued apace after his election, with, for example, repeated references to "criminal aliens" and the labeling of African nations as "shithole countries." As with his previous xenophobic statements and policies, commentators wondered how the president could make such blatantly offensive statements and enact such controversial policies without paying a heavy political price. But the reason for the political success of Trump's xenophobic statements and policies is relatively straightforward: there is a high level of xenophobia among rank-and-file Republicans. In 2014, among those who self-identified as Republicans, two thirds scored above the sample mean on the xenophobia index. By the time of the 2018 survey, it was even higher, with 83 percent of self-identified Republicans scoring above the sample average on xenophobia. This undoubtedly reflects Trump's influence on the party, as well an exodus of former Republicans who do not support such positions. It also reflects a fascinating dynamic outside of the Grand Old Party (GOP): decreasing levels of xenophobia among all Americans who are not Republicans.

We have asked the same questions as part of the xenophobia battery across multiple waves of the fear surveys, and the changes between 2014 and 2018 show a strong shift away from xenophobic attitudes among Americans who identify as political independents or Democrats (see Figure 6.1). The full scale has seven questions, with response options ranging from 0 (least xenophobic response) to 3 (most xenophobic response), so the full summed scale ranges from 0 to 21. In the 2014 survey, self-identified Republicans averaged 12.3, which decreased slightly to 11.6 in 2016, then stayed basically the same at 11.7 in 2018. Separating out those who identify as "strong Republicans" from those who said they were "moderate Republicans" or "lean Republican" shows that xenophobia has also decreased slightly among moderate and leaning Republicans; meanwhile, it has actually increased slightly among those who self-identify as "strong Republicans."

In contrast to Republicans, xenophobic sentiment decreased dramatically among both self-identified political independents and Democrats between 2014 and 2018. Among independents, the average score on the xenophobia index was 10.7 in 2014, 9.7 in 2016, and then 7.5 in 2018. Among Democrats, the average score has also fallen steadily, from 8.6 in 2014 to 4.1 in 2018. The number is even lower among those who identify as "strong Democrats" (from 8.3 in 2014 to 3.0 in 2018).

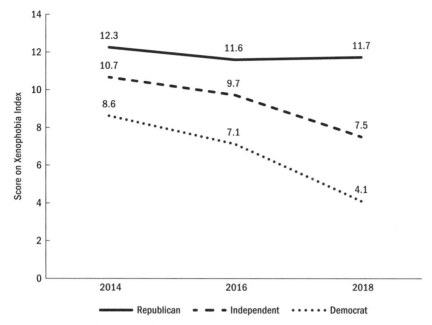

Figure 6.1. Xenophobia by Political Party Identification, 2014–2018.

These trends show two clear "Trump effects." First, Trump was able to win the 2016 election as a result of appealing to the xenophobic sentiment among Republican primary voters and also fear of the outsider among political moderates and even some Democrats (particularly in Rust Belt and Sun Belt states). Second, Trump's efforts to pursue hardline immigration policies such as the Muslim travel ban, family separation, and efforts to build his long-promised border wall have ultimately produced a backlash among political independents and liberals, who now show more xenophilic attitudes toward immigrants than they did previously.

Finally, in 2018 we asked Americans whether Trump generally made them feel afraid or hopeful, angry or proud. Feelings about Trump are direct reflections of levels of xenophobia, which far outpaced even political orientation (conservative to liberal) and political party identification in its predictive power for feelings about Trump (see Figure 6.2). Similarly, xenophobia (or, in this case, xenophilia) was the strongest

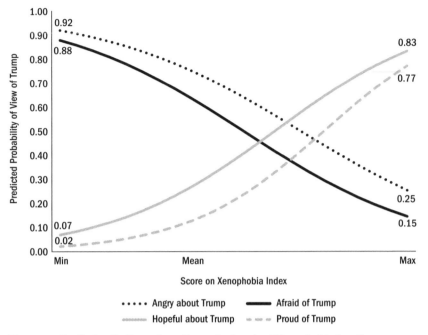

Figure 6.2. Predicting Feelings about Trump by Levels of Xenophobia (2018).

predictor of whether respondents said the GOP more generally made them feel angry and afraid. Trump's rise to power is inseparable from his anti-immigrant rhetoric and policies, and his electoral success and efforts at governance have, in turn, had a profound effect on patterns and levels of xenophobia among the American public. Trump is a politician who thrives on fear, also benefiting from the fear he generates.

None of this, of course, is to say that xenophobia is a new phenomenon in American history or politics. The politics of travel bans and border walls fall neatly into a long line of fearful "nativist" responses to new immigrants in the United States.[25] Nonetheless, Trumpism represents an important cultural shift in American politics, away from "dog whistle" tactics about race and ethnicity to a more overt "bullhorn" strategy that targets "immigrants" in general rather than specific groups of people. This, in effect, allows politicians and members of the public to espouse racist ideas and policies while claiming plausible (or, at least, rhetorical) deniability from charges of racism. The combination of xenophobia and punitiveness has proved to be an effective electoral strategy, particularly in primary elections for socially conservative parties, where xenophobic positions are unlikely to alienate large shares of the electorate. Conservative politicians at every level will undoubtedly take note of Trump's successes and follow suit. At the same time, a pro-immigrant backlash is also underway. Consequently, the politics of fears about "outsiders" are sure to be front and center in American life for the foreseeable future.

## Fear for Your Well-Being

The social consequences of specific forms of fear such as conspiracism, xenophobia, and fear of crime are myriad. But what are the consequences of fear more generally for the individuals who are afraid? To evaluate this question, we used the "Sum of All Fears" measure we introduced at the beginning of the book. To see how fearfulness affects a person's overall well-being, we looked at the relationship between scores on the Sum of All Fears and levels of anxiety, as well as the relationship with personal satisfaction in the following areas: life in general, financial situation, family life, social life, mental health, physical health, and even personal appearance. Fearfulness has a profound effect on well-being in *all these areas*.

We created an anxiety index based on questions about whether, during the past two weeks, respondents had felt nervous, worried uncontrollably, had difficulty sleeping, were restlessness, easily irritable, or felt that something terrible was going to happen to them.[26] Overall levels of fear were strongly tied to levels of anxiety. The relationship is steady and linear, such that increased fear corresponds with increased anxiety. To get a picture of how overall levels of fear were connected to personal well-being, we collapsed the Sum of All Fears measure into categories for those who were low in fear (one standard deviation or more below the sample mean), mid-low in fear (between one standard deviation below the sample mean and the mean), mid-high (between the sample mean and one standard deviation above the mean), and high in fear (more than one standard deviation above the sample mean). Among those at the lowest levels of fear, only 23 percent were above the sample mean on anxiety. In comparison, 35 percent and 54 percent of respondents scored above the mean on anxiety at mid-low and mid-high levels of

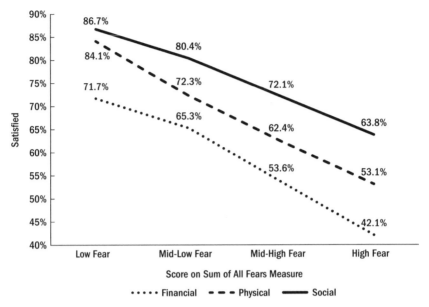

Figure 6.3. Satisfaction with Finances, Physical Health, and Social Life by Levels of Fear (2018).

fear, respectively. Among those with the highest levels of overall fear, 76 percent scored above the sample mean on levels of anxiety. In a very real sense, anxiety is a cognitive response to fear.[27] Consequently, increases in fear correspond to similar increases in anxiety and are accompanied by its noxious consequences for health and well-being.[28]

Likewise, overall levels of fear were the strongest predictor of levels of life satisfaction when compared to sociodemographic, political, and religious predictors. The Sum of All Fears index significantly predicted each of the specific indicator questions about satisfaction with different aspects of life. Figure 6.3 shows some of the negative relationships between levels of fear and quality of life. At the lowest levels of fear, there were high levels of satisfaction with social life (87 percent), physical health (84 percent), and financial situation (72 percent). As levels of fear increased, each quality-of-life indicator declined precipitously. For those well above the sample mean on overall levels of fear, satisfaction with social life (64 percent), health (53 percent), and money (42 percent) was much lower. Interestingly, overall levels of fear had the strongest relationship to levels of satisfaction with one's personal appearance, followed by financial situation, physical health, and then mental health. Fearfulness had the weakest (but still significant) relationship to the level of satisfaction with family life. Overall, levels of fear are strongly associated with decreased health, life satisfaction, and general well-being across a wide range of domains.

For those unfortunate enough to suffer from excess amounts of fear, there is yet another thing to fear: the punishing toll of fear itself on health and well-being. In the evolutionary sense, fear has unquestionably had positive benefits for survival. But in the contemporary world, increased levels of fear are detrimental for optimal cognitive functioning, personal well-being, and communal health. Indeed, our fears even keep us from enjoying public events such as concerts and sporting events. Nearly a quarter of respondents said they avoid going to public venues out of fear of terrorism. Instead, we feel safer in our homes and trade live music and seats on the 50-yard line for watching events on television and streaming video in isolation.

So what are we to do? How can we reduce our level of fear in the digital age? We end with some advice for reducing your level of fear.

# Conclusion

*Where Do We Go from Fear?*

Throughout this book, we have detailed and examined a wide range of fears held by Americans in the early twenty-first century. Fear can be partisan or personal, rooted in past experience, or something we only hear about on the news. Fear can be about specific targets, people, or concerns. It can also be a vague sense of unease and dread about the present and future. Regardless of its form, fear is pervasive, persistent, and pernicious. It also has important but underappreciated implications for understanding social and political behavior.[1]

Fears among the public are both diverse and commonplace. Many fears reflect political concerns and are the product of narrowcast media whose raison d'être is stoking fears accompanied by anger and a perceived righteousness that affirms particular political worldviews by denigrating others. Although some fears among the public are primarily partisan, we also found that many nonpartisan fears can be examined in conjunction. The patterns in our catch-all Sum of All Fears measure showed that social location—meaning the variety of different social statuses a person holds—strongly influences overall levels of fear. Individuals who occupy more vulnerable social statuses are more exposed to and at greater risk of having high levels of fear. This increased exposure to fear is a product of social inequality, but it also deepens inequality, robbing millions of people of their well-being and quality of life. In this way, we can see that fear has clear sociological dimensions, in addition to its better-understood psychological dimensions.

The natural world provides plenty of grist for the fear mill. With the United Nations warning that the impact of global warming will cause widespread cataclysm by 2040, that fears over the environment are rising along with global temperatures is not surprising.[2] From wildfires and droughts to hurricanes and floods, natural disasters are expected to grow more frequent and severe. Unfortunately, fear of natural disasters does not motivate preparedness among the vast majority of the public. As a society, we are much better at pulling together to deal with the aftermath of a destructive hurricane than we are at planning in advance to minimize the danger. Store shelves emptied of bottled water, food, and essentials, along with gas stations without fuel, are a common sight on the eve of a hurricane. Bare store shelves and fuel storages are a prepper's worst nightmare. A small, but growing, subculture in America, preppers are ready for severe weather, a natural disaster, an economic collapse, or even the end of the world as we know it. For the preppers we met in Chapter 3, fear is managed through preparedness. Although most Americans would say that preppers go too far, a lesson is to be learned from the prepping community: Don't wait until it's too late. Preppers like to say, "If you fail to prepare, then prepare to fail." Many also warn not to come knocking on their doors when you run out of supplies because preppers also plan to defend their preps.

Our research shows that belief in conspiracy theories is rooted in fear and is quite common among the public. Fully one out of every three Americans were willing to believe in the conspiratorial government cover-up of the South Dakota crash, something we made up and that they had never heard of before. But it is a mistake to see conspiratorial thinking as only happening among those who are deranged. Conspiratorial Gnosticism holds great appeal as a meaningful worldview and enraptures many intelligent, well-intentioned people. This is particularly the case in the age of the Internet, which has facilitated the popularity and spread of conspiracy theories. By the time of our surveys, only one out of four Americans did *not* believe in any conspiracy theories. Just as it is unwise to see conspiratorial beliefs as uncommon, seeing belief in these immense webs of misinformation as harmless amusements is also a mistake.

Although writing off the fever dreams of a conspiratorial Svengali like Alex Jones as something destined to inhabit only the fringes of society is tempting, his immense audience—including the 45th president of the United States—shows the potential power conspiracies have to influence mainstream social institutions. Conspiracy theories poison public discourse and form a severe impediment to civic engagement and sound governance. Beyond these considerable social consequences, conspiracism can deepen individuals' levels of anxiety, even to the point of purchasing weapons and, in extreme cases, carrying out acts of violence against innocent people. For the worse, conspiratorial Gnosticism is here to stay, and we must reckon with how to counter the spread and influence of the misinformation and disinformation that drives these all-encompassing belief systems.

The threat of a terror attack, or becoming the victim of such an attack, causes us to pay close attention to media coverage of these events. Unfortunately, this gives terror groups the very exposure that fuels more attacks. Moreover, our fears not only grow with the amount of media consumed but are also shaped by the specific forms of media we use. Thus, regular viewers of cable news and local TV not only fear terrorism more than readers of a daily newspaper; they also fear different and specific violent extremists. Where we get our news predicts whether we fear jihadis, white supremacists, or Antifa, to name a few. Similarly, the fear of being a mass shooting victim is also increased by our patterns of media usage. We are not only complicit in manufacturing our own fears when we tune in to news coverage of mass shootings and terror attacks, but we are contributing to the spread of hateful messages and giving killers the notoriety they seek. In this regard, we have argued that people can take charge of their fears by reducing media usage or turning away from coverage that is sensational or glorifies violence.

Fear of crime is more about *perceptions* of crime than realities of crime. This is evident in the very strong relationship between projected fears about religious evil and fears about crime. Even more directly, we demonstrated that perceptions of crime are quite often at odds with actual rates of crime. The mismatch between the perception and the reality of crime reflects the law of inverse proportionality regarding media coverage of crime: The rarer, stranger, and more sensational the crime, the more media attention it will receive. Perceiving that crime has gotten worse (even when it was getting better) drives Americans' seemingly insatiable desire for harsher criminal punishment. Likewise, fears about foreigners and immigrants are key drivers of support for punitive social policies, particularly among white Americans. Mass incarceration in the

United States is the end result of an extended period of extremely high levels of support for retributive criminal justice among the American public, a view rooted in irrational fear.

Harsh criminal justice policies and practices are not the only social and political consequences of fear. Fears about "outsiders" also undermine the basic social trust that provides the interactive glue for inclusive and protective communities. This is ironic given that fear of outsiders has played an important role in communal solidarity throughout humans' evolutionary history. But in modern, diverse societies, the fear of people who are not like us has severe consequences for communities and out-groups and very little upside. Furthermore, as the example of support for Donald Trump—as well as other populist politicians throughout the world and American history—shows, fears about immigrants are the preferred province of demagogues. The power and potential political consequences of fears about foreigners and immigrants are not to be underestimated.

In the end, the consequences of fear are as widespread and vast as fear itself. Wherever fear is found, there are consequences for the individuals who are afraid, as well as for others in their communities. But why is fear so pervasive if its effects are so often negative? To understand fear's ubiquity despite its considerable range of ill effects, we must return to the neurology of fear. Now, based on the wide range of findings from our research, we are in a much better position to connect the neurobiology of threat detection to the range of subjective experiences of fear. In short, it is time to bring fear back to where it all starts: the human brain.

## Primordial Fear in the Digital Age

Fear is multivalent, omnipresent, and instinctual. The rapid detection of environmental threats is a key component of survival and evolution—not just for humans but for all mammals. The fact that we humans share with other animals the fundamental dimensions of the threat detection systems that underlie fear is a testament that "fear is central to mammalian evolution" and to the evolutionary advantage of being able to quickly detect threats and respond with defensiveness and vigilance.[3] But the basic features of humanity's threat detection systems that are a boon for evolutionary fitness and survival can be become the bane of existence, particularly in instances where cognitive processes are routinely hijacked by unnecessary fears. Cutting-edge neuroscience about the brain's threat detection and defense systems that underlie our conscious experiences of fear helps us understand the broad patterns of fear we find in studies of the public.

A key finding from experimental research about detecting threats— such as snakes and potentially hostile people—is that the brain and body's systems for accomplishing this operate efficiently, automatically, and at an unconscious level.[4] In a sense, threat detection is like breathing; it continues apace without our conscious control. These features make fear less immune to conscious manipulation than other emotional responses. This feature has important implications for the clinical treatment of disorders involving fear and its close cognitive cousin, anxiety.[5]

Another important implication of the automaticity of humans' threat detection systems is that they are highly prone to false positives. The evolutionary logic is uncomplicated. Playing it safe and reacting to a perceived snake that turns out to be just a stick is better than blithely ignoring a perceived branch that turns out to be a diamondback. Consequently, "perceptual systems are biased toward discovering threat" and "rely on a quick and dirty process that rather risks false positives than false negatives."[6] This makes sense for the long-term survival of a species. But when our long-bred perceptual systems are exposed to new environments, particularly in an age of incessant visual stimulation, they may routinely lead us astray. Worse yet, they may hound our consciousness into pathological disorders.[7]

Not only are the threat detection systems that undergird experiences of fear prone to false positives; they also, by design, *command* cognitive attention.[8] Again, the evolutionary logic is relatively simple. A potential threat that is not given due cognitive diligence may be the last one you ever experience. Better safe than sorry—or dead. But in a digital world of perpetual media consumption—where attention-getting is the name of the game—the cognitive command of fear is an exploitable feature of our neurological circuitry. From horror films and heavy metal music to MSNBC and Fox News, not to mention

Facebook, Twitter, and your local news, fear sells. Often there is an evolutionary reason for social virality in the digital age. As media consumers, we must recognize that our innate threat detection systems are always attuned to their environment and—to the extent it is possible— attempt to bring manipulative efforts to hold our attention through fear and sensationalism to the surface of conscious reflection, where they can be evaluated more rationally and discarded if they are misleading or unwanted.

In addition to the extensive use of fear by various forms of media, personal experiences of fear leave long-lasting impressions on our brains. Fearful memories are particularly vivid and intransigent. Again, there is a good evolutionary reason for this, as learning from a close encounter with danger can be an important source of future survival. But entrenched memories of threatening experiences can become psychologically and socially damaging. Indeed, "many human mental disorders—including anxiety, phobia, post-traumatic stress syndrome and panic attack—involve malfunctions in the brain's ability to control fear."[9] As a result, fear is a key component of understanding and effectively treating a wide range of psychological disorders.

Beyond these psychological connections to the neurological underpinnings of fear, a number of social and political phenomena can be better understood by considering the neurobiological processes that drive fear. Consider xenophobia. We have shown how xenophobia relates to punitiveness, fear of other people, and demagoguery, which preys on these fears. But we have not addressed why the fear of foreigners is so *widespread*. Given that the United States was in no way facing an unprecedented immigration crisis during the period of our surveys, why were so many Americans deeply fearful of immigrants? In short, because it is an effective way to solidify in-group loyalties by harnessing humans' ingrained fear of people outside their own group.[10] More crassly, because it works politically. This is especially the case when there is a perceived economic and political threat, such that opposing partisans are seen as enemies to be combatted rather than fellow citizens with whom to form coalitions.[11] As with so many other forms of fear, narrowcast media can exacerbate fears about foreigners and be exploited by shameless politicians more interested in electoral success than fairness, accuracy, or human dignity.[12]

Managing Fear

Fear is a double-edged sword. It can keep us safe from harm and motivate us to take action to address potentially harmful future events such as climate change. But all too often fears are unfounded, unnecessary, and psychologically, socially, and politically damaging. Consequently, *managing* fear is important for all of us as individuals, as well as for the health and well-being of our communities. To that end, we conclude with some considerations for dealing with fear in an ever-changing digital age.

All things considered, the evolutionary advantages of the brain's threat detection systems can often betray us in the era of the Internet, constant media streaming, and smartphones.[13] Is it any wonder that anxiety disorders are strongly connected to Internet and cell phone use?[14] The world, of course, will only continue to grow ever more connected and digitized. As this happens, we must consciously and vigilantly take the reins of our primordial fears. But doing so is dependent on the extent to which we are aware of how fear operates and how it can be used manipulatively. Fear cannot be banished; it can only be managed. Doing so well is no small task, but it is necessary to live your best life and to make our communities better.

Although we have detailed some of the primary ways that fear is encoded in our biology and how this affects the ways fear is experienced and used, perhaps the most hopeful finding from the neuroscience research on fear is that, while humans' basic threat-detection systems operate automatically, fear must also be understood within a "two-system" framework.[15] To control our fears, we must make use of not only our expanding knowledge about the physiological and neurological pathways of threat detection (the first system) but also our conscious recognition and processing of fear (the second system). Some of the triggering processes of fear may be unconscious, but we can nonetheless make these aspects *part of our conscious understanding* of our experiences and perceptions of fear. So, how do we manage our fear in the era of the 24-hour news cycle, Facebook alerts, and hyperbolic Twitter feeds?

First, avoid overtly partisan media. Although it might be cognitively satisfying to have your political worldview validated through such outlets, the long-term costs far outweigh the short-term benefits of perceived righteousness. In contrast, being willing to listen to different points of view—earnestly rather than facilely—is difficult in the short term, but it has long-term benefits for individuals and communities.

Limit screen time and smartphone use. Disengaging from incessant media consumption is a necessary step to limiting the fear and anxiety that accompany the constant use of screens. You can also take practical steps to improve the manner in which you consume media when you do use screens, such as not setting alerts on electronic devices for news. This Pavlovian training can only increase your sense of anxiety. Slow news will not hurt you. In fact, getting information this way will help you reason through the stories of the day with deliberative cognition and, by extension, decrease your anxiety level compared to compulsive media consumption.

Be skeptical of claims that all people from a particular category—be it immigrants, political opponents, or racial and religious minorities—are uniformly bad. Such claims are propaganda and clearly do not reflect the complex reality and diversity actually found among people from different groups. Although the "isms" of the world are often expressed as anger, they are ultimately rooted in fear.

Face your fears. Extinguishing fear comes about by removing the negative associations attached to particular targets of perceived threat. *Learn* about the things you are afraid of, as increasing knowledge about topics engages "cool," deliberative cognition rather than the "hot," intuitive cognition that drives fear.

Plan for future fears, such as natural disasters and climate change, within reason. Preparation and training for negative events allow us to manage fear in the short term and respond appropriately when disaster does strike.

Always remember that news media will disproportionately show you the most violent, unusual, and strange acts of humanity, while typically ignoring that which is kind, commonplace, and mundane. Remember that the law of inverse proportionality governs what will be covered in the news, regardless of the source of the information.

Learn to recognize conspiratorial thinking when you see it. You can do this by asking some basic questions, such as: Are there connections between disparate events being made too easily? Are the voices of a particular narrative about shadowy forces at play in the world closed off to disconfirming evidence? Are difficult and complex issues being glossed over in favor of sweeping theories about all of history and society? If the answer to each of these questions is "yes," seek out new sources of information about the topic of interest and regard information from such conspiratorial sources with the utmost skepticism.

Be on guard and vigilant against the use of fear to manipulate you to purchase products or vote for particular parties or candidates. We must be governed by reasonableness, not paranoia.

Do not let fear undermine your trust in other people. Withdrawal and isolation enhance fear, while sociality reduces it. Connect with your neighbors and friends, and be willing to make connections with people across social boundaries, such as political party, race, ethnicity, sexuality, and age. Diverse contacts expand your view of the world and keep the narrow suspicions of fear at bay.

More generally, when you feel afraid but are able to recognize that there is *no* imminent danger, do not allow fear to be the master of your mind. Conquering fear means seizing the reigns of thought back from our impetuous senses, which are well meaning but ever on guard against a threat. That is, after all, their biological and cognitive function. Consequently, managing fear well means being able to deliberatively assess and dismiss the many false positives produced by our age-old threat-detection systems.

When you feel afraid and it turns out that your fear *is* well founded, actively engaging ways to ameliorate the threat is the best course of action. Notably, however, engaging *social* sources of threats is critical. After all, these are the only sources of fear we can reasonably have any hope of affecting. At the level of social policy, this requires a sober assessment of the actual realities of fear rather than relying merely on perceptions of fear.[16] Fear-motivated activism can be effective, so long as the object of fear is genuinely threatening and assessed deliberatively. Taking action against perceived threats that are not actually threatening is counterproductive and ineffective. Furthermore, like irrational fear itself, policy based on misguided perceptions of threat is likely to cause more problems than it solves.

Importantly, all these suggestions require considerable effort on our part. All are easier said than done. Fear, the product of deep historical and evolutionary time, is ingrained in our brains. Managing it properly is not simple or easy. But knowing what fear is and how it works, we can position ourselves to respond to it in ways that limit its potential to harm us. Amending the famous words of the 32nd president of the United States, which have never been truer than they are today, we can say that, although there are many useful aspects of fear, the greatest danger is ironically posed by fear itself.

## ACKNOWLEDGMENTS

The authors are grateful to so many people who made the Chapman University Survey of American Fears possible. At Chapman, we'd like to thank President Daniele Struppa, Provost Glenn Pfeiffer, and Dean Patrick Fuery for their unwavering support of the fear project and of the Earl Babbie Research Center, at which the survey is based.

Mr. David C. Henley and Mrs. Ludie Henley generously support the Henley lab where so many of our students worked and where much of this research was conducted.

We'd like to thank Sheri Ledbetter, who made it her personal mission to bring fear research to the public. Her public relations campaign spanned the globe and was the most successful in the university's history. She brought fear to every state in the nation via television, radio, and the Internet, helping us to educate the public.

Student researchers have been part of this project from the beginning, and we couldn't have done it without them. We'd like to thank Otneil Pavia, Cassidy Rawlinson, Tyler Jones, Brett Robertson, Matt Lyons, Kunal Sharma, Shreya Sheth, Natalie Gallardo, Kai Hamilton-Gentry, Brittney Souza, Andrew Calloway, Sarah LeMay, Roanan Keldin, and Annika Ford.

And to all the students who helped develop the scope and depth of the items through Chris Bader's Interterm Survey Course—here are the results of your efforts. We are grateful for your work.

Joseph Baker's work on this project was generously supported by a noninstructional assignment from the College of Arts & Sciences at East Tennessee State University in the spring of 2017. Thanks to Bill Duncan, Gordon Anderson, and Bert Bach for supporting the sabbatical and this research.

Waves 1 through 3 of the survey were conducted by GfK, and we'd like to thank the GfK team members for their dedication to the project and their leadership in the field of survey methods.

SSRS conducted Waves 4 and 5 of the survey, and thanks are due to Robyn Rapoport, Kyle Berta, and the whole team for their attention to detail and commitment to rigorous methodology.

Finally, all four authors must thank their respective better halves, Sara Bader, Amy Edmonds, Michelle Miller-Day, and David Shafie, for their endless patience as we delved into the world of fear.

# NOTES

INTRODUCTION

1 Crimesider Staff 2017.
2 Lee 2015.
3 Associated Press 2017.
4 Lee and Nguyen 2015.
5 Morain 2015.
6 Spakovsky and Landsman 2015.
7 Moons 2015.
8 Elinson 2017.
9 Stevens, Fuller, and Dickerson 2017.
10 Peele 2016.
11 Emslie 2017.
12 Cf. Adelman et al. 2017; Ousey and Kubrin 2009, 2014.
13 Bersani 2014.
14 "Mother of Woman Killed" 2015.
15 Thomas and Thomas 1928.
16 Glassner 1999.
17 Tiedens and Linton 2001.
18 Brader 2005.
19 Stafford, Chandola, and Marmot 2007; Pearson and Breetzke 2014.
20 Bazargan 1994; Krause 1991.
21 Robinson et al. 2003; Skogan 1986.
22 Altheide 2006; Furedi 2006; Nacos, Block-Elkon, and Shapiro 2011.
23 Glassner 1999.
24 See Jarymowicz and Bar-Tel 2006; Learner and Keltner 2001; Öhman and Mineka 2001.
25 Robin 2004; Nacos et al. 2011; Tudor 2003; Furedi 2006.
26 Hankiss 2001.
27 LeDoux 2003.
28 LeDoux 2014:2871.
29 LeDoux 2017.
30 LeDoux and Brown 2017:E2023.
31 LeDoux and Hofmann 2018:67.
32 Sinclair 2017.

33 Solon 2017.
34 Newport 2017a.
35 Gallagher 2017.
36 Newport 2017b.
37 The CSAF is not a panel study. Each year involves a different, cross-sectional sample of Americans.
38 For technical details about the development of the survey and its administration, please see the online appendix at http://www.thearda.com/fear/.

CHAPTER 1. THE SUM OF ALL FEARS
1 We also asked several other questions designed to gauge skepticism or acceptance of the need for vaccinations. Each question asked respondents to indicate their level of agreement with a statement about vaccinations. The additional statements included "Many of my friends are concerned with the side effects of vaccinations," "Parents should have the right to decide which vaccinations their children receive," and "Vaccinating children helps to protect them from illnesses." Respondents indicated their level of agreement using possible responses of "strongly agree," "agree," "disagree," or "strongly disagree."
2 Geggel 2017.
3 Hiltzik 2014.
4 Poindexter and Esquivel 2014.
5 See, for example, the Pew Research Center's research on social media usage (Greenwood, Perrin, and Duggan 2016).
6 The final scale has high internal reliability, with a Cronbach's $\alpha$ = .81. Responses were coded such that higher values equated to greater skepticism about vaccines.
7 Becker 1963:149. Also see Gusfield 1955.
8 Our religion measures included affiliation (Protestant, Catholic, "just Christian," and other compared to those with no religion), frequency of religious service attendance, how religious the person considers him- or herself to be, and whether the respondent has a "literalist" view of the Bible.
9 Kaplan 2015.
10 For the following analyses we utilized the 2017 survey, which contained a more comprehensive battery of politically charged items, for reasons that will become clear.
11 We asked respondents to provide their religious affiliation and coded those responses into categories for "Protestant," "Catholic," "just Christian," "Jewish," "other religion," "agnostic," "nothing at all," and "atheist."
12 The complete set of possible answers included "extremely liberal," "liberal," "leaning liberal," "moderate," "leaning conservative," "conservative," and "extremely conservative."
13 Our conservative fear items included one that is inherently tied to race, asking respondents how much they fear "whites no longer being the majority in the United

States." We ran another version of this model excluding this item, and doing so did not change the pattern of results. All effects remained significant, and African Americans remained less afraid of conservative issues.

14  Gardner 2009:138–140.
15  Marcus, Neuman, and Mackuen 2000:45–64.
16  Brader 2005:398–401.
17  Clinton 2008.
18  Hunter, Meares, and Ginn 2018:121–126.
19  Iyengar, Peters, and Kinder 1982.
20  Cf. Callanan 2012; Chiricos, Eschholz, and Gertz 1997; Chiricos, Padgett, and Gertz 2000; Eschholz, Chiricos, and Gertz 2003; Kort-Butler and Sittner Hartshorn 2011; Nellis and Savage 2012.
21  Gil de Zuniga, Correa, and Valenzuela 2012.
22  DellaVigna and Kaplan 2007; Hopkins and Ladd 2014.
23  Feldman et al. 2012.
24  But there are certainly plenty of losers, such as democracy and civic society.
25  Farhi 2003.
26  Cronbach's α = .89. We also scaled the final variable so that its minimum was zero (final range 0 to 33.14).
27  The same pattern is evident in Wave 2 data between frequency of religious service attendance and overall levels of fear. Similarly, with regard to religious identity, the lowest average scores on the Sum of All Fears index in Wave 4 were found among Protestants (−1.27), followed by atheists (−0.63).
28  Ellis and Wahab 2013; Jong and Halberstadt 2016.
29  Downey 1984.
30  Jong et al. 2017.
31  Baker, Stroope, and Walker 2018; Galen and Kloet 2011.
32  Allport and Ross 1967; Eisinga, Felling, and Peters 1990; Hall, Matz, and Wood 2010. Different aspects of religiosity—such as fundamentalism and "quest" orientation—effectively have countervailing effects on prejudice (see Altemeyer and Hunsberger 1992).
33  Baker and Draper 2010; Bader, Baker, and Mencken 2017; Bader, Baker, and Molle 2012.
34  Baker, Bader, and Mencken 2017.
35  Cf. Cossman and Rader 2011; Franklin, Franklin, and Fearn 2008; Jackson 2008; Skogan and Maxfield 1981; Wynne 2008.
36  Cf. Hollander 2001; Rader 2008; Reid and Konrad 2004.
37  Cossman and Rader 2001.
38  McKee and Milner 2000.
39  May 2001; Pain 2000; Rader, Cossman, and Porter 2012.
40  Rader et al. 2012:135.
41  Franklin et al. 2008.
42  Franklin et al. 2008:207.

CHAPTER 2. THINGS ARE NOT WHAT THEY SEEM

1 *The Gospel of Thomas*, or *The Hidden Sayings of Jesus*, saying 5, verses 1 and 2 (Meyer 2005:8).

2 *We Never Went to the Moon* is the title of a popular book about Apollo moon landing conspiracies by Bill Kaysing (2017).

3 Note that many of Johnston's claims about his career, particularly his time with NASA and its contractors, have been called into question by skeptics.

4 Cf. Nevett 2017.

5 See King 2003.

6 We capitalize "Truth" throughout the chapter when referring to the beliefs of conspiracists because this how they themselves understand and articulate it. Although it may seem ironic that "Truth" is the focal point of conspiracy subcultures, this is an inevitable result of the labeling of conspiracy beliefs as a form of stigmatized *knowledge*.

7 Williams 1996:27.

8 See Franks, Bangerter, and Bauer 2013; Ward and Voas 2011.

9 See de Young 1997; Victor 1993.

10 Robertson 2016.

11 Cf. Byford 2011; Goode and Ben-Yehuda 2009. Surprisingly, the intimate connections and parallels between moral panics and conspiracy theories have previously gone unnoticed by scholars of each.

12 Butter 2014.

13 Knight 2002.

14 On resistance identities in the context of global capitalism, see Castells (2010).

15 Welch 2006.

16 Byford 2011.

17 Byford 2011:132.

18 Accordingly, conspiracy believers have significantly higher levels of dualistic, Manichean thinking (Oliver and Wood 2014a).

19 Butter 2014:20–21.

20 Barkun 2003.

21 Goertzel 1994:740; Zarefsky 1984:72.

22 Campbell 2008.

23 On folk devils and their related social processes of solidarity, see Cohen (2002).

24 Mason 2002; Melley 2002.

25 Goldberg 2001:260.

26 Barkun 2003; Dean 1998; Pipes 1997.

27 Indeed, a recurrent theme of conspiracy narratives is the idea that the conspirators will use subtle clues, signs, and symbols that could reveal the conspiracy. For example, conspiracy theories about the Denver airport claim that the Illuminati included Masonic symbols, odd paintings, and gargoyles throughout the airport as a hidden sign of their presence. Why conspirators who ostensibly want to hide their activities also choose to reveal them is never made clear.

28  Obviously, here, we refer to the fact that there is not a preexisting claim about a conspiracy about a "South Dakota crash" rather than the factual truth behind any of the conspiracy theories we discuss.

29  We coded respondents as believing in a conspiracy theory if they agreed or strongly agreed with the relevant statement.

30  We also controlled for xenophobia and paranormalism in this analysis, which is discussed later in this chapter.

31  Overall, and by far, the strongest predictor of believing in the South Dakota crash conspiracy was paranormalism. We will dig deeper into these connections shortly.

32  From the mean to one standard deviation above the mean.

33  From one to two standard deviations above the mean.

34  More than two standard deviations above the mean.

35  Anxiety and vigilance are two cognitive tendencies triggered by human responses to abstract threats (see Eilam, Izhar, and Mort 2011).

36  Goldberg 2001:240.

37  Respondents were again coded as believing in a conspiracy if they agree or strongly agreed with the statement that "The government is concealing what it knows about . . ." X.

38  Cf. Goertzel 1994.

39  We counted those at one standard deviation and above as having the highest levels of fear.

40  Belief in Satan as the cause of evil was a more powerful predictor than all the demographic and religious factors but was not as powerful a predictor as xenophobia, paranormalism, or fear.

41  On defining the paranormal, see Bader, Baker, and Mencken (2017) and Baker, Bader, and Mencken (2016).

42  Respondents used the possible responses "strongly disagree," "disagree," "agree," and "strongly agree."

43  This relationship holds when belief in the UFO conspiracy is excluded from the conspiracy index and belief in aliens is excluded from the paranormal index. The correlation between the conspiracy count and paranormalism index is 0.35 when UFOs and aliens are included and .31 when they are excluded from the measures. So while the overlap between ufology and conspiracism is an important aspect of this connection, it is not driving the relationship. Rather, there is clearly a more general relationship between paranormalism and conspiracism that goes beyond this specific subculture.

44  Bader et al. 2017.

45  People have sighted strange objects in the sky throughout history. What has changed is the interpretation of the phenomena. Biblical accounts of strange objects in the sky are identified as the work of angels. A series of mysterious "airships" sighted across the United States in the late nineteenth century were believed to be the work of eccentric inventors. Arnold's sighting marked a turning point wherein the prominent explanation for such events was extraterrestrial.

46 Barker 1956.

47 See Bader et al. (2017) for a deeper dive into the inner workings of the UFO movement.

48 Near the beginning of his talk at Contact in the Desert 2018, radio personality Jimmy Church introduced David Wilcock. To thunderous applause, Church yelled, "Science is now behind us! If one more domino falls we will know that we were all right."

49 Robertson 2016:170.

50 Robertson 2016:195.

51 Robertson 2016:200.

52 For the remainder of our discussion of Wilcock's claims, we will state those claims as if they were factual to avoid the continual repetition of terms such as allegedly and purported.

53 Wilcock also noted that Hitler was the "illegitimate son of British royalty" who had been planted in Germany to foster a war that the Illuminati wanted.

54 Butter 2012.

55 Web traffic and demographic details are from Quantcast, "Infowars.com," retrieved May 1, 2018, www.quantcast.com.

56 See Infowars.com (2017) and Stack (2016).

57 Transcribed from an interview of Jones in *New World Order* (2009), a documentary directed by Luke Meyer and Andrew Neel and produced by SeeThink Films.

58 See Williamson 2018.

59 On the differences between the New World Order and birther conspiracies with regard to Obama, see Butter (2012).

60 Kwong 2017. Corsi left InfoWars in June 2018 and has since sued Alex Jones for defamation, claiming Jones and others on the platform—including Trump political operative Roger Stone—publicly questioned Corsi's sanity after he stopped working for InfoWars. Conspiracy subcultures are unsurprisingly suffused with paranoia and infighting, even among former allies.

61 Rosenberg 2017.

62 Rosenberg 2016.

63 Goldman 2016.

64 Interview with Seth Jackson, in *New World Order* 2009.

65 *New World Order* 2009.

66 Transcribed from InfoWars radio show, October 16, 2015.

67 Quotes are transcribed from InfoWars radio show from December 2, 2015. Video of the interview has since been removed from YouTube but can still be readily found online.

68 Megyn Kelly interview with Alex Jones. *NBC News*, June 17, 2017.

69 Raymond 2018.

70 On cognitive dissonance and ideology, see Festinger (1957).

71 The 2018 survey did not ask about Obama's birth certificate. We did ask about this conspiracy in 2016 and received the same general pattern of results when using this measure in place of belief in school shooting conspiracies in the 2016 data.

72 On the importance of Islamophobia to Trump voting in 2016, see Whitehead, Perry, and Baker (2018).

73 *New World Order* 2009.

74 Butter 2014; Hofstadter [1952] 2008.

75 Aupers 2012.

76 Vosoughi, Roy, and Ara 2018.

77 Becker, Alzahabi, and Hopwood 2013; Woods and Scott 2016.

78 Butter 2014.

79 Piketty 2014.

80 DiGrazia 2017.

81 Hacker and Pierson 2010.

CHAPTER 3. APOCALYPSE HOW?

1 The term *survivalist* has fallen out of favor due to its negative association with the militia movement and the likes of Timothy McVeigh, the Oklahoma City bomber. *Prepper* is the preferred nomenclature.

2 Austen 2018a.

3 Austen 2018b.

4 The following are observations by Ann Gordon.

5 Forstchen 2009.

6 U.S. Congress 2009.

7 This is a pseudonym to protect his confidentiality.

8 "Prepper Camp 2018™," class schedules and map. accessed February 20, 2018, www.preppercamp.com.

9 Sanchez 2018; Sanchez, Shah, and Santiago 2018.

10 Rice 2018.

11 Friedman 2017.

12 Reed et al. 2015.

13 Grossman 2015.

14 Live Science Staff 2012.

15 Harvey 2018.

16 Malo 2018.

17 Slavo 2017.

18 Prepper Shows USA 2018.

19 Dennis and Eilperin 2017.

20 Flesher and Biesecker 2017.

21 Kennedy 2016.

22 Colvin 2017.

23 Smith, Kim, and Son 2017.

24 See Kinane and Ryan (2009) and Hall (2009).

25 Many world figures have been named as the Antichrist, including Gorbachev, Reagan, Obama, and nearly every pope.

26 Bivins 2008.

27 Aveni 2016.

28 Festinger, Riecken, and Schachter [1956] 2008.

29 Pappas 2011.

30 Aveni 2016.

31 Wojcik 1997:121.

32 Wojcik 1997:121.

33 Bever 2018.

## CHAPTER 4. BEYOND CONTAGION

1 Interviewed in Showtime's (2017) *American under Fire*, "San Bernardino, California."

2 Straub, Zeunik, and Gorban 2017.

3 Interviewed in Showtime's (2017) *American under Fire*, "San Bernardino, California."

4 Fenton, Celona, and Golding 2016.

5 Zarembo 2016.

6 Thatcher 1985.

7 Beckmann, Dewenter, and Thomas 2017.

8 Kissell 2015.

9 Kostinsky, Bixler, and Kettl 2001.

10 Lankford and Tomek 2018; Towers et al. 2015.

11 Meindl and Ivy 2017:368.

12 Associated Press 2018.

13 Fernandez, Turkewitz, and Bidgood 2018.

14 Pappas 2017.

15 Meindl and Ivy 2017.

16 Hamilton 2017.

17 McClatchy-Tribune News Service 2018.

18 Marcus, Neumann, and MacKuen 2000:11.

19 Callanan 2012.

20 Wendling 2018.

21 Zimmerman, Ryan, and Duriesmith 2018:1.

22 Janik 2018.

23 Janik 2018.

24 Kimmel and Mahler 2003.

25 "Q & A with Our Founders" 2018.

26 On fame-seeking rampage shooters, which are more common in the United States than other countries, see Lankford (2016b).

27 Lankford and Madfis 2018.

28   "Q & A with Our Founders" 2018.
29   "The Plan" n.d.
30   "Don't Say Their Name" 2016.
31   Vales 2016.
32   Wemple 2015.
33   Wemple 2015.
34   Meindl and Ivy 2017:369.
35   These findings are based on a series of regression analyses that also controlled for demographic characteristics such as partisanship, gender, and education.
36   Jamieson and Capella 2008:179–180, emphasis added.
37   Jamieson and Capella 2008:237.
38   Fisher 2017.
39   Love 2017.
40   Ahmed and Matthes 2016.
41   Powell 2011, 2018.
42   Bail 2012, 2014.
43   Edgell, Gerteis, and Hartmann 2006.
44   Edgell et al. 2016.
45   Uddin and Pantzer 2018.
46   Mitchell and Toner 2016.
47   Yazdiha 2014:268.
48   Kishi 2017.
49   DeFoster 2015:75.
50   Takim 2011.
51   Bowe and Makki 2016.
52   Montopoli 2010. The quote used is slightly different than the one in the news story because we transcribed the encounter between Ramsey and his constituents using video footage.
53   Smietana 2014.
54   Whitehead, Perry, and Baker 2018.
55   We did not specify which national newspapers respondents read. That regular readers of a daily national newspaper are less likely to favor extra screening at airports and are more comfortable with mosques being built in their neighborhoods, but that they are slightly more likely to view Muslims as terrorists is interesting to note.
56   Morris 2007:707.
57   Differences are statistically significant, even when controlling for social and religious characteristics, as well as political partisanship. Full results are available at http://www.thearda.com/fear/.
58   Placing all the measures asking about fear of Muslims and those asking about fear of immigrants into a single factor analysis produces only one factor no matter what type or rotation is specified.
59   Lankford 2016a.
60   Fisher and Keller 2017; Lankford 2016c.

61 Miller, Azrael, and Hemenway 2002; Miller, Hemenway, and Azrael 2007; Siegel, Ross, and King 2013.

62 Wallace 2015.

63 This relationship holds even after accounting for social characteristics and political identity. There is also a significant positive relationship between fear of mass shootings and fear of gun control.

CHAPTER 5. VISIONS OF CRIME

1 Doubek 2018.

2 Doubek 2018.

3 Hurst 2018.

4 Alvarez and Buckley 2013.

5 For an excellent review of the research literature, see Lane et al. (2016).

6 Rader 2007.

7 See Denham (2016).

8 There are different definitions of a serial killer. Some definitions require that an individual kill two individuals to qualify, others three. Some definitions further require the killings to occur with a time separation between them for the killer to qualify as a serial killer. The Radford/FGCU database defines a serial killer as someone who murders at least two victims.

9 Aamodt 2015. Notably, there may be some time lag effects in the recognition of active serial killers. Still, the evidence is clear that the number has decreased over time.

10 Gallup 2018.

11 Gramlich 2018.

12 Violent crime rates are from the Uniform Crime Report produced by the Federal Bureau of Investigation (2017). In 2017 the violent crime rate was 382.9. In 1987, the violent crime rate was 612.5. The rate is per 100,000 people, so in 2017 there were 382.9 violent crimes for every 100,000 people in the United States. The number of serial killers operating in 1987 was 172 according to the Radford University/ FGCU Serial Killer Database.

13 A key consideration in survey research is the length of time the survey requires. The longer the survey takes, the more likely it is that respondents will either stop partway or begin checking boxes randomly or without thought.

14 Rountree and Land 1996.

15 Full results of regression analyses available at http://www.theArda.com/Fear.

16 Lane et al. 2016.

17 Lane et al. 2016:119.

18 Cf. Ferraro 1996; Warr 1984.

19 Morgan and Kena 2017.

20 Oudekerk and Truman 2017.

21 Cf. Rader, Cossman and Porter 2012; Scarborough et al. 2010.

22 Age could be considered as a physical vulnerability, such as when older persons are physically unable to defend themselves, or a social vulnerability, such as when young persons lack the economic resources to deal with adverse events.

23 For causes of death for young black men, see "Leading Causes of Death by Age Group, Black Males—United States 2015*," www.cdc.gov. For causes of death for young black women, see "Leading Causes of Death by Age Group, Black Females—United States 2015*," www.cdc.gov. Accessed November 12, 2018.

24 Petrosky et al. 2017.

25 See Table 3 in Petrosky et al. 2017.

26 Sorensen, Manz, and Berk 1998. We must note here that homicide is not the same as murder. A homicide has occurred when a person has killed another person. This would include, for example, a case where a person accidentally killed another. Murder is a type of homicide wherein it is believed that one *intended* to kill another person. Most often, prosecutors will charge a person with murder if that crime is also assumed to have involved premeditation.

27 This finding is not unique to the United States. For example, Hestermann (2016) found that German media outlets are far more likely to report on crimes that involve young female victims.

28 Cohen 2002.

29 See ABC News (2012). Note that the additional crimes cited by this article are not further cannibalistic attacks but a wide range of crimes and behaviors including suicide, running a drug ring, discharging a firearm, and killing a neighbor's goat.

30 See Palamar (2018) for an excellent overview of the phenomenon.

31 The complete scale included "never," "less than once a month but at least once a year," "once or twice a month," "once or twice a week," "most days," and "every day."

32 For example, previous research has noted the importance of asking about fear of specific offenses when analyzing fear of crime (cf. Kohm et al. 2012) and a wide variety of media types/channels (cf. Chiricos, Escholz, and Geertz 2003). A key addition to the current project was the inclusion of multiple measures of religiosity in our analyses since we have found certain aspects of religion, particularly beliefs about religious evil, are related to fear of crime.

33 Cf. Chiricos, Eschholz and Gertz 1997; Chiricos, Padgett, and Gertz 2000.

34 Pew Research Center 2013.

35 Analyses of the effects of fictional and true-crime TV viewing are from the first wave of the CSAF, which was the only wave to include these items. Previous research that has examined the effects of fictional crime shows has been mixed (cf. Eschholz, Chiricos and Gertz 2003; Kort-Butler and Sittner Hartshorn 2011). The effects of viewing true crime shows on fear of crime were much stronger and more robust than fictional crime shows, but viewing programs such as *CSI* still had a significant positive effect on overall fear of crime.

36 See, for example, Roche, Pickett, and Gertz (2016).

37 Cf. Roche et al. 2016; Weitzer and Kubrin 2004.

38 Cavender and Bond-Maupin 1993.

39 Baker and Booth 2016.

40 Morone (2003) provides an overview of how theologically conservative religious views about sin and damnation have inspired social movements and influenced American politics throughout history.

41 King James Version.

42 Matthews, Johnson, and Jenks 2011.

43 For instance, Rader et al. (2012) analyze the predictors of fear of crime using the Panel Study on American Religion and Ethnicity but do not even mention, let alone test, whether or how religion affects fear of crime.

44 Lee and Ulmer 2000:1184.

45 See Applegate et al. 2000; Bader et al. 2010; Unnever, Cullen, and Applegate 2005.

46 We coded the religious affiliations of our respondents into major categories, including Protestant, Catholic, Christian (neither Protestant nor Catholic), Jewish, other religions, agnostic, and no religion. Atheists were the contrast category in our analyses.

47 See Baker (2008) on patterns of belief in religious evil. See Bivins (2008) on the uses of fear about religious evil in evangelical Protestantism.

48 This effect for views of the Bible is only apparent after controlling for political identity. In a bivariate context, there is not a significant relationship between views of the Bible and fear of crime. After accounting for the fact that biblical literalists are much more likely to be politically conservative, the suppressor effect showing the moderate protective influence of biblical literalism becomes significant.

49 Bonn 2014.

50 Lane et al. 2016.

51 Rader and Haynes 2014.

52 Skogan 1995.

53 Cordner 2010.

54 Enns 2014, 2016.

55 The Cronbach's α score for the index was .87, indicating high internal reliability.

56 These percentages are from the 2018 CSAF.

57 Results of one-way analysis of variance (ANOVA) predicting scores on the punitiveness index by fear of crime broken into quartiles for white respondents only ($F = 6.077$; $p < .001$).

58 Baker, Cañarte, and Day 2018.

59 Moore and Shepherd 2007; Rengifo and Bolton 2012; Robinson et al. 2003.

60 Adams and Serpe 2000; Hale 1996; Skogan 1986.

61 Britto, Van Slyke, and Francis 2011.

62 Skogan 1986; Woldoff 2006.

63 Sampson, Raudenbush, and Earls 1997.

64 We dichotomized each item such that 1 equals finding that the respondent has engaged in the behavior in question. We summed these items to create a count variable for community engagement that ranges from 0 to 9 with a Cronbach α = .84.

65 Other factors included perceived crime in the neighborhood, general life satisfaction, the presence of social support networks, and previous victimization.

66 We are grateful for F. Carson Mencken for suggesting this relationship and his advice about running the final analyses.

67 Garofalo 1981:856.

68 See also Jackson and Gray (2010).

69 DuBow, McCabe, and Kaplan 1980.

70 Garofalo 1981:856.

71 Garofalo 1981:856.

72 Jackson and Gray 2010; see also Liska and Warner 1991.

73 Jackson and Gray 2010; see also Tallis, Davey, and Capuzzo 1994.

74 Britto et al. 2011; Ditton and Innes 2005.

75 Markowitz et al. 2001.

76 Some have suggested that public education campaigns about the actual amount of crime and the risk it poses might be effective (see Lane et al. 2016).

77 Lipschultz and Hilt 2002.

## CHAPTER 6. CONSEQUENCES OF FEAR

1 On the relationship between personal health and conspiratorial ideation, see Oliver and Wood (2014b).

2 Hofstadter [1952] 2008.

3 Hetherington 2005; Jennings and Stoker 2004; Newton 2001; Putnam 2001.

4 Jolley and Douglas 2014; Oliver and Wood 2014a.

5 In this model we used the full conspiracy belief index, which has answer choices from 1 (strongly disagree) to 4 (strongly agree) for each of the 10 conspiracies queried. This allows us to preserve more variance in conspiratorial ideology for the purposes of graphing the outcome, and for comparing the strength of conspiracism as a predictor to other variables.

6 The predicted probability of buying a gun out of fear at the lowest levels of the full conspiracy theory belief index was .05, compared to .21 for those at the maximum level of conspiracism.

7 In support of the hypothesis that the Internet, in general, and greater digital connectivity, specifically, facilitate the spread of conspiracy theory, there is a very strong relationship between the frequency of cell phone use per day and the number of conspiracies that respondents believed. Those who used their phones at least 7 hours a day believed in an average of two more conspiracy theories than did respondents who used their phones less than an hour a day.

8 Gerbner and Gross 1976.

9 See Gerbner et al. 1978, 1979, 1980.

10 See Gerbner et al. 1980.

11 Morgan and Shanahan 2010.

12 Ferrise 2018.

13 Other personal characteristics come into play, although their effects are far less pronounced. Older people are more likely to accept help as are those who report a race other than white, black, or Hispanic. Southerners, conservatives, and African Americans feel less safe receiving help from strangers. Catholics, Protestants, and those who are simply uncertain as to the nature of God feel less safe taking help, but those who attend religious services more frequently are more likely to accept help.

14 Older people also reported greater willingness to help, as do those who attend religious services more frequently.

15 Ruddell and Urbina 2004; Wang 2012.

16 Sundstrom and Kim 2014; Wimmer 1997.

17 Baker, Cañarte, and Day 2018:365.

18 Hamlin et al. 2013.

19 Mahajan and Wynn 2012.

20 See, for example, Brannigan (1998) and Hickel (2014).

21 Amend 2018.

22 Whitehead, Perry, and Baker 2018.

23 In the 2018 data, the Cronbach's α score (.94) for the xenophobia index is actually higher after including the questions about support for Trump's travel ban and border wall.

24 Woodward 2018.

25 On xenophobia in American immigration policies throughout history, see Bennett (1988), Curran (1975), and Kanstroom (2007).

26 The anxiety scale had high internal reliability, with a Cronbach's α = .93.

27 See Öhman (2008).

28 The relationships among levels of fear, life satisfaction, and anxiety remain strong and significant after controlling for the sociodemographic, religious, and political predictors of fears.

CONCLUSION

1 Marcus, Neuman, and MacKuen 2000.

2 Davenport 2018.

3 Öhman and Mineka 2001:483.

4 Öhman 2005; Öhman et al. 2007; Öhman and Mineka 2001.

5 See Dymond et al. (2015) and Öhman (2008).

6 Öhman 2008:712; Öhman and Mineka 2001:487.

7 Maren 2005.

8 Öhman 2009; Öhman, Flykt, and Esteves 2001.

9 LeDoux 2002:63–64.

10 See Öhman, Lundqvist, and Esteves (2001) and Olsson et al. (2005).

11 Iyengar and Westwood 2015.

12 In a model predicting xenophobia as the outcome, the strongest predictors were political ideology and frequency of viewing Fox News.

13 The problematic use of smartphones is significantly correlated with fear, particularly the "fear of missing out" (Wolniewicz et al. 2018).

14 Jenaro et al. 2007; Lepp, Barkley, and Karpinski 2014.

15 LeDoux and Pine 2016.

16 Sunstein 2005.

# REFERENCES

Aamodt, Mike G. 2015. "Serial Killer Statistics." Accessed November 5, 2018. http://maamodt.asp.radford.edu.

ABC News. 2012. "Face-Eating Cannibal Attack May Be Latest in String of 'Bath Salts' Incidents." *ABC News*, June 1. Accessed October 15, 2018. www.abcnews.com.

Alvarez, Lizette, and Cara Buckley. 2013. "Zimmerman Is Acquitted in Trayvon Martin Killing." *New York Times*. Accessed September 18, 2018. www.nytimes.com.

Adams, Richard E., and Richard T. Serpe. 2000. "Social Integration, Fear of Crime, and Life Satisfaction." *Sociological Perspectives* 43(4):605–629.

Adelman, Robert, Lesley Williams Reid, Gail Markle, Saskia Weiss, and Charles Jaret. 2017. "Urban Crime Rates and the Changing Face of Immigration: Evidence across Four Decades." *Journal of Ethnicity in Criminal Justice* 15(1):52–77.

Ahmed, Saifuddin, and Jörg Matthes. 2016. "Media Representation of Muslims and Islam from 2000 to 2015: A Meta-analysis." *International Communication Gazette* 79(3):219–244.

Allport, Gordon W., and J. Michael Ross. 1967. "Personal Religious Orientation and Prejudice." *Journal of Personality and Social Psychology* 5(4):432–443.

Altemeyer, Bob, and Bruce Hunsberger. 1992. "Authoritarianism, Religious Fundamentalism, Quest, and Prejudice." *International Journal for the Psychology of Religion* 2(2):113–133.

Altheide, David. 2006. *Terrorism and the Politics of Fear.* Lanham, MD: AltaMira Press.

Alvarez, Lizette, and Cara Buckley. 2013. "Zimmerman Is Acquitted in Trayvon Martin Killing." *New York Times*. Accessed September 18, 2018. www.nytimes.com.

Amend, Alex. 2018. "Analyzing a Terrorist's Social Media Manifesto: The Pittsburgh Synagogue Shooter's Posts on Gab." *Southern Poverty Law Center* Accessed October 28, 2018. www.splcenter.org.

Applegate, Brandon K., Francis T. Cullen, Bonnie S. Fisher, and Thomas Vander Ven. 2000. "Forgiveness and Fundamentalism: Reconsidering the Relationship between Correctional Attitudes and Religion." *Criminology* 38(3):719–754.

Associated Press. 2017. "How the Kate Steinle Case Became an Immigration Flashpoint." *Chicagotribune.com*, December 3. Accessed February 21, 2018. www.chicagotribune.com.

Associated Press. 2018. "High Schoolers Posing as Columbine Shooters Suspended." *Yahoo! News*, November 2. Accessed November 3, 2018. www.yahoo.com.

Aupers, Stef. 2012. "Trust No One: Modernization, Paranoia, and Conspiracy Culture." *European Journal of Communication* 27(1):22–34.

Austen, Jane. 2018a. "PrepTorial™ How to Make a Survival Bidet for Home and Travel." *Survivor Jane*. Accessed February 20, 2018. www.survivorjane.com.

Austen, Jane. 2018b. ""No Way Am I Ever Giving up Toilet Paper!!"—Famous Last Words. (Caution: Potty Talk!!)." *Survivor Jane*. Accessed February 20, 2018. www.survivorjane.com.

Aveni, Anthony. 2016. *Apocalyptic Anxiety: Religion, Science, and America's Obsession with the End of the World*. Boulder: University Press of Colorado.

Bader, Christopher, Joseph O. Baker, and F. Carson Mencken. 2017. *Paranormal America: Ghost Encounters, UFO Sightings, Bigfoot Hunts, and Other Curiosities in Religion and Culture*, 2nd edition. New York: NYU Press.

Bader, Christopher, Joseph O. Baker, and Andrea Molle. 2012. "Countervailing Forces: Religiosity and Paranormal Belief in Italy." *Journal for the Scientific Study of Religion* 51(4):705–720.

Bader, Christopher D., Scott A. Desmond, F. Carson Mencken, and Byron R. Johnson. 2010. "Divine Justice: The Relationship between Images of God and Attitudes Toward Criminal Punishment." *Criminal Justice Review* 35(1):90–106.

Bail, Christopher A. 2012. "The Fringe Effect: Civil Society Organizations and the Evolution of Media Discourse about Islam since the September 11th Attacks." *American Sociological Review* 77(6):855–879.

Bail, Christopher A. 2014. *Terrified: How Anti-Muslim Fringe Organizations Became Mainstream*. Princeton, NJ: Princeton University Press.

Baker, Joseph O. 2008. "Who Believes in Religious Evil? An Investigation of Sociological Patterns of Belief in Satan, Hell, and Demons." *Review of Religious Research* 50(2):206–220.

Baker, Joseph, Christopher D. Bader, and F. Carson Mencken. 2016. "A Bounded Affinity Theory of Religion and the Paranormal." *Sociology of Religion* 77(4):334–358.

Baker, Joseph O., and Alexis L. Booth. 2016. "Hell to Pay: Religion and Punitive Ideology among the American Public." *Punishment & Society* 18(2):151–176.

Baker, Joseph O., David Cañarte, and L. Edward Day. 2018. "Race, Xenophobia, and Punitiveness among the American Public." *Sociological Quarterly* 59(3):363–383.

Baker, Joseph O., and Scott Draper. 2010. "Diverse Supernatural Portfolios: Certitude, Exclusivity, and the Curvilinear Relationship between Religiosity and Paranormal Beliefs." *Journal for the Scientific Study of Religion* 49(3):413–424.

Baker, Joseph O., Samuel Stroope, and Mark H. Walker. 2018. "Secularity, Religiosity, and Health: Physical and Mental Health Differences between Atheists, Agnostics, and Nonaffiliated Theists Compared to Religiously Affiliated Individuals." *Social Science Research* 75:44–57.

Barker, Gray. 1956. *They Knew Too Much about Flying Saucers*. New York: University Books.

Barkun, Michael. 2003. *A Culture of Conspiracy: Apocalyptic Visions in Contemporary America*. Berkeley: University of California Press.

Bazargan, Mohsen. 1994. "The Effects of Health, Environmental, and Socio-Psychological Variables on Fear of Crime and Its Consequences among Urban Black Elderly Individuals." *International Journal of Aging and Human Development* 38(2):99–115.

Becker, Howard S. 1963. *Outsiders: Studies in the Sociology of Deviance*. New York: The Free Press.

Becker, Mark W., Reem Alzahabi, and Christopher J. Hopwood. 2013. "Media Multi-tasking Is Associated with Symptoms of Depression and Social Anxiety." *Cyberpsychology, Behavior, and Social Networking* 16(2):132–135.

Beckmann, Klaus B., Ralf Dewenter, and Tobias Thomas. 2017. "Can News Draw Blood? The Impact of Media Coverage on the Number and Severity of Terror Attacks." *Peace Economics, Peace Science and Public Policy* 23(1):1–14.

Bennett, David H. 1988. *The Party of Fear: From Nativist Movements to the New Right in American History*. Chapel Hill: University of North Carolina Press.

Bersani, Bianca E. 2014. "An Examination of First and Second Generation Immigrant Offending Trajectories." *Justice Quarterly* 31(2):315–343.

Bever, Lindsey. 2018. "The Making of The Doomsday Clock: Art, Science and the Atomic Apocalypse." *Washington Post*, January 25.

Bivins, Jason C. 2008. *Religion of Fear: The Politics of Horror in Conservative Evangelicalism*. New York: Oxford University Press.

Bonn, Scott. 2014. *Why We Love Serial Killers*. New York: Skyhorse.

Bowe, Brian J., and Taj W. Makki. 2016. "Muslim Neighbors or an Islamic Threat? A Constructionist Framing Analysis of Newspaper Coverage of Mosque Controversies." *Media, Culture & Society* 38(4):540–558.

Brader, Ted. 2005. "Striking a Responsive Chord: How Political Ads Motivate and Persuade Voters by Appealing to Emotions." *American Journal of Political Science* 49(2):388–405.

Brannigan, Augustine. 1998. "Criminology and the Holocaust: Xenophobia, Evolution, and Genocide." *Crime & Delinquency* 44(2):257–276.

Britto, Sarah, David M. Van Slyke, and Teresa I. Francis. 2011. "The Role of Fear of Crime in Donating and Volunteering: A Gendered Analysis." *Criminal Justice Review* 36(4):414–434.

Butter, Michael. 2012. "The Birthers' New World Order: Conspiracy Theories about Barack Obama." Pp. 225–246 in *Obama and the Paradigm Shift: Measuring Change*, edited by Birte Christ and Greta Olson. Heidelberg: Universitätsverlag Winter.

Butter, Michael. 2014. *Plots, Designs, and Schemes: American Conspiracy Theories from the Puritans to the Present*. Berlin: De Gruyter.

Byford, Jovan. 2011. *Conspiracy Theories: A Critical Introduction*. London: Palgrave Macmillan.

Callanan, Valerie J. 2012. "Media Consumption, Perceptions of Crime Risk and Fear of Crime: Examining Race/Ethnic Differences." *Sociological Perspectives* 55(1): 93–115.

Campbell, Joseph. 2008. *The Hero with a Thousand Faces*, 3rd edition. Novato, CA: New World Library.

Castells, Manuel. 2010. *The Power of Identity* (The Information Age: Economy, Society and Culture, Volume II), 2nd edition. Malden, MA: Wiley.

Cavender, Gray, and Lisa Bond-Maupin. 1993. "Fear and Loathing on Reality Television: An Analysis of 'America's Most Wanted' and 'Unsolved Mysteries.'" *Sociological Inquiry* 63(3):305–317.

Centers for Disease Control. 2018. "Leading Causes of Death (LCOD) by Age Group, Black Females—United States, 2015." https://www.cdc.gov/health equity/lcod /women/2015/black. Accessed November 12, 2018.

Centers for Disease Control. 2018. "Leading Causes of Death (LCOD) by Age Group, Black Males—United States, 2015." https://www.cdc.gov/health equity/lcod /men/2015/black. Accessed November 12, 2018.

Chiricos, Ted, Sarah Eschholz, and Marc Gertz. 1997. "Crime, News and Fear of Crime: Toward an Identification of Audience Effects." *Social Problems* 44(3):342–357.

Chiricos, Ted, Kathy Padgett, and Marc Gertz. 2000. "Fear, TV News and the Reality of Crime." *Criminology* 38(3):755–785.

Clinton, Hillary. 2008. "3 AM White House Ringing Phone." *YouTube*, May 15. Accessed July 14, 2018. www.youtube.com/watch?v=7yr70dFUARg.

Cohen, Stanley. 2002. *Folk Devils and Moral Panics: The Creation of the Mods and the Rockers*, 3rd edition. New York: Routledge.

Colvin, Jill. 2017. "Under Trump, Climate Change not a National Security Threat." *Chicago Tribune*, December 18.

Cordner, Gary. 2010. *Reducing Fear of Crime: Strategies for Police*. Washington, DC: Office of Community Oriented Policing Services.

Cossman, Jeralynn S., and Nicole E. Rader. 2011. "Fear of Crime and Personal Vulnerability: Examining Self-Reported Health." *Sociological Spectrum* 31(2):141–162.

Crimesider Staff. 2017. "'Help Me, Dad': Father Recounts Kate Steinle's Last Moments on San Francisco Pier." *CBS News*, October 24. Accessed February 21, 2018. www.cbsnews.com.

Curran, Thomas J. 1975. *Xenophobia and Immigration, 1820–1930*. Boston: Twayne Publishers.

Davenport, Coral. 2018. "Major Climate Report Describes a Strong Risk of Crisis as Early as 2040." *New York Times*, October 8.

Dean, Jodi. 1998. *Aliens in America: Conspiracy Cultures from Outerspace to Cyberspace*. Ithaca, NY: Cornell University Press.

DeFoster, Ruth. 2015. "Orientalism for a New Millennium: Cable News and the Specter of the 'Ground Zero Mosque.'" *Journal of Communication Inquiry* 39(1):63–81.

DellaVigna, Stefano, and Ethan Kaplan. 2007. "The Fox News Effect: Media Bias and Voting." *Quarterly Journal of Economics* 122(3):1187–1234.

Denham, Jack. 2016. "The Commodification of the Criminal Corpse: 'Selective Memory' in Posthumous Representations of Criminal." *Mortality* 21(3):229–245.

Dennis, Brad, and Juliet Eilperin. 2017. "EPA Dismisses Half of Key Board's Scientific Advisers; Interior Suspends More Than 200 Advisory Panels." *Washington Post*, May 8.

de Young, Mary. 1997. "The Devil Goes to Day Care: McMartin and the Making of a Moral Panic." *Journal of American Culture* 20(1):19–25.

DiGrazia, Joseph. 2017. "The Social Determinants of Conspiratorial Ideation." *Socius* 3:1–9. https://journals.sagepub.com/doi/pdf/10.1177/2378023116689791.

Ditton, Jason, and Martin Innes. 2005. "The Role of Perceptual Intervention in the Management of Crime Fear." Pp. 595–624 in *Handbook of Crime Prevention and Community Safety*, edited by Nick Tilly. Portland, OR: Willand Publishing.

"Don't Say Their Name: Media Struggles with Reporting on Orlando Gunman." 2016. *NPR*, June 15. Accessed October 29, 2018. www.npr.org.

Doubek, James. 2018. "Black Teenager Shot At after Asking for Directions." *NPR*. Accessed August 10, 2018. www.npr.org

Downey, Ann M. 1984. "Relationship of Religiosity to Death Anxiety of Middle-Aged Males." *Psychological Reports* 54(3):811–822.

DuBow, Fred, Edward McCabe, and Gail Kaplan. 1980. *Reactions to Crime: A Critical Review of the Literature*. Washington, DC: U.S. Department of Justice, Law Enforcement Assistance Administration, National Institute of Law Enforcement and Criminal Justice.

Dymond, Simon, Joseph E. Dunsmoor, Bram Vervliet, Bryan Roche, and Dirk Hermans. 2015. "Fear Generalization in Humans: Systematic Review and Implications for Anxiety Disorder Research." *Behavior Therapy* 46(5):561–582.

Edgell, Penny, Joseph Gerteis, and Douglas Hartmann. 2006. "Atheists as "Other": Moral Boundaries and Cultural Membership in American Society." *American Sociological Review* 71(2):211–234.

Edgell, Penny, Douglas Hartmann, Evan Stewart, and Joseph Gerteis. 2016. "Atheists and Other Cultural Outsiders: Moral Boundaries and the Non-Religious in the United States." *Social Forces* 95(2):607–638.

Eilam, David, Rony Izhar, and Joel Mort. 2011. "Threat Detection: Behavioral Practices in Animals and Humans." *Neuroscience and Biobehavioral Reviews* 35(4): 999–1006.

Eisinga, Rob, Albert Felling, and Jan Peters. 1990. "Church Involvement, Prejudice and Nationalism: A Research Note on the Curvilinear Relationship between Church Involvement and Ethnocentrism in the Netherlands." *Review of Religious Research* 31(4):417–433.

Elinson, Zusha. 2017. "Illegal Immigrant's Acquittal in San Francisco Killing Draws Backlash." *Wall Street Journal*, December 1. Accessed February 21, 2018. www.wsj.com.

Ellis, Lee, and Eshah H. Wahab. 2013. "Religiosity and Fear of Death: A Theory-Oriented Review of the Empirical Literature." *Review of Religious Research* 55(1):149–189.

Emslie, Alex. 2017. "BLM Ranger Tells Jury How His Gun Was Stolen before Steinle Killing." *KQED News*, October 26. Accessed February 21, 2018. https://ww2.kqed.org.

Enns, Peter K. 2014. "The Public's Increasing Punitiveness and its Influence on Mass Incarceration in the United States." *American Journal of Political Science* 58(4):857–872.

Enns, Peter K. 2016. *Incarceration Nation: How the United States Became the Most Punitive Democracy in the World*. New York: Cambridge University Press.

Eschholz, Sarah, Ted Chiricos, and Marc Gertz. 2003. "Television and Fear of Crime: Program Types, Audience Traits, and the Mediating Effect of Perceived Neighborhood Racial Composition." *Social Problems* 50: 395–415.

Farhi, Paul. 2003. "Everybody Wins." *American Journalism Review* (April 1):32–36.

Federal Bureau of Investigation. 2017. *2017: Crime in the United States*. Accessed November 5, 2018. https://ucr.fbi.gov.

Feldman, Lauren, Edward Maibach, Connie Roser-Renouf, and Anthony Leiserowitz. 2012. "Climate on Cable: The Nature and Impact of Global Warming Coverage on Fox News, CNN, and MSNBC." *International Journal of Press/Politics*. 17: 3-31.

Fenton, Reuven, Larry Celona, and Bruce Golding. 2016. "How Hero Bar Owner Helped Cops Catch Chelsea Bombing Suspect." *New York Post*, September 20. https://nypost.com.

Fernandez, Manny, Julie Turkewitz, and Jess Bidgood. 2018. "For 'Columbiners,' School Shootings Have a Deadly Allure." *New York Times*, May 30. Accessed October 22, 2018. www.nytimes.com.

Ferraro, Kenneth F. 1996. "Women's Fear of Victimization: Shadow of Sexual Assault?" *Social Forces* 75(2):667–690.

Ferrise, Adam. 2018. "Video, Witnesses: Man Attacks Woman, Man who Stopped to Help Him before Deputy Shoots Him on I-90." *Cleveland.com*, May 25. Accessed October 27, 2018. www.cleveland.com.

Festinger, Leon. 1957. *A Theory of Cognitive Dissonance*. Stanford, CA: Stanford University Press.

Festinger, Leon, Henry W. Riecken, and Stanley Schachter. [1956] 2008. *When Prophecy Fails: A Social and Psychological Study of a Modern Group that Predicted the Destruction of the World*. London: Pinter & Martin.

Fisher, Max, and Josh Keller. 2017. "What Explains U.S. Mass Shootings? International Comparisons Suggest an Answer." *New York Times*, November 7.

Fisher, Tyler. 2017. "Our Left-Right Media Divide Told through Charlottesville." *POLITICO*, October 24. Accessed October 29, 2018. www.politico.com.

Flesher, John, and Michael Biesecker. 2017. "Trump Administration Moves to Withdraw Clean-Water Rule." Associated Press, June 27.

Forstchen, William R. 2009. *One Second After*. New York: Forge.

Friedman, Lisa. 2017. "For EPA Chief, Discussing Climate after Storm Is 'Insensitive.'" *New York Times*, September 12.

Franklin, Travis W., Cortney A. Franklin, and Noelle E. Fearn. 2008. "A Multilevel Analysis of the Vulnerability, Disorder, and Social Integration Models of Fear of Crime." *Social Justice Research* 21(2):204–227.

Franks, Bradley, Adrian Bangerter, and Martin W. Bauer. 2013. "Conspiracy Theories as Quasi-Religious Mentality: An Integrated Account from Cognitive Science, Social Representations Theory, and Frame Theory." *Frontiers in Psychology* 4:1–12.

Furedi, Frank. 2006. *Culture of Fear Revisited*. London: Continuum.

Galen, Luke W., and James D. Kloet. 2011. "Mental Well-Being in the Religious and the Non-Religious: Evidence for a Curvilinear Relationship." *Mental Health, Religion & Culture* 14(7):673–689.

Gallagher, Katie. 2017. "Would You Live in a Haunted House?" *Trulia*, October 5. Accessed October 31, 2018. www.trulia.com.

Gallup, Inc. 2018. "Crime." *Gallup.com*. Accessed November 5, 2018. https://news .gallup.com.

Gardner, Daniel. 2009. *The Science of Fear*. New York: Plume.

Garofalo, James. 1981. "The Fear of Crime: Causes and Consequences." *Journal of Criminal Law and Criminology* 72(2):839–857.

Geggel, Laura. 2017. "'Vast Majority' of Online Anti-vaxxers Are Women." LiveScience, December 29. Accessed May 21, 2018. www.livescience.com.

Gerbner, George, and Larry Gross. 1976. "Living with Television: The Violence Profile." *Journal of Communication* 26(2):173–99.

Gerbner, George, Larry Gross, Marilyn Jackson-Beeck, Suzanne Jeffries-Fox, and Nancy Signorielli. 1978. "Cultural Indicators: Violence Profile No. 9." *Journal of Communication* 28(3): 176–207.

Gerbner, George, Larry Gross, Michael Morgan, and Nancy Signorielli. 1980. "The 'Mainstreaming' of America: Violence Profile No. 11." *Journal of Communication* 30(3):10–29.

Gerbner, G., Larry Gross, Nancy Signorielli, Michael Morgan, and Marilyn Jackson-Beeck. 1979. "The Demonstration of Power: Violence Profile No. 10." *Journal of Communication* 29(3):177–196.

Gil de Zuniga, Homero, Teresa Correa, and Sebastian Valenzuela. 2012. "Selective Exposure to Cable News and Immigration in the U.S.: The Relationship Between FOX News, CNN, and Attitudes toward Mexican Immigrants." *Journal of Broadcasting & Electronic Media* 56(4): 597–615.

Glassner, Barry. 1999. *The Culture of Fear: Why Americans Are Afraid of the Wrong Things*. New York: Basic Books.

Goertzel, Ted. 1994. "Belief in Conspiracy Theories." *Political Psychology* 15(4):731–742.

Goldberg, Robert A. 2001. *Enemies Within: The Culture of Conspiracy in Modern America*. New Haven, CT: Yale University Press.

Goldman, Adam. 2016. "The Comet Ping Pong Gunman Answers Our Reporter's Questions." *New York Times*, December 7.

Goode, Erich, and Nachman Ben-Yehuda. 2009. *Moral Panics: The Social Construction of Deviance*, 2nd edition. Malden, MA: Wiley-Blackwell.

Gramlich, John. 2018. "5 Facts about Crime in the U.S." *Pew Research Center*, January 30. Accessed November 5, 2018. www.pewresearch.org.

Greenwood, Shannon, Andrew Perrin, and Maeve Duggan. 2016. "Social Media Update 2016." *Pew Research Center: Internet, Science & Tech*, November 11. Accessed May 22, 2018. www.pewinternet.org.

Grossman, Lisa. 2015. "Floods that Hit New York City Every 500 Years Now Hit Every 24." *New Scientist*, September 28. Accessed Oct. 31. 2018. www.newscientist.com.

Gusfield, Joseph R. 1955. "Social Structure and Moral Reform: A Study of the Woman's Christian Temperance Union." *American Journal of Sociology* 61(3):221–232.

Hacker, Jacob S., and Paul Pierson. 2010. *Winner-Take-All Politics: How Washington Made the Rich Richer—and Turned Its Back on the Middle Class.* New York: Simon & Schuster.

Hale, Chris. 1996. "Fear of Crime: A Review of the Literature." *International Review of Victimology* 4(2):79–150.

Hall, Deborah L., David C. Matz, and Wendy Wood. 2010. "Why Don't We Practice What We Preach? A Meta-Analytic Review of Religious Racism." *Personality and Social Psychology Review* 14(1):126–139.

Hall, John R. 2009. *Apocalypse: From Antiquity to the Empire of Modernity.* Cambridge, UK: Polity Press.

Hamlin, J. Kiley, Neha Mahajan, Zoe Liberman, and Karen Wynn. 2013. "Not Like Me = Bad: Infants Prefer Those Who Harm Dissimilar Others." *Psychological Science* 24(4):589–94.

Hamilton, Matt. 2017. "Families of San Bernardino Attack Victims Accuse Facebook, Google and Twitter of Aiding Terrorism in Lawsuit." *Los Angeles Times*, May 3.

Hankiss, Elemér. 2001. *Fears and Symbols: An Introduction to the Study of Western Civilization.* Budapest: Central European Press.

Harvey, Chelsea. 2018. "Scientists Can Now Blame Individual Natural Disasters on Climate Change." *E&E News: Scientific American*, January 2. Accessed November 3, 2018. www.scientificamerican.com.

Hestermann, Thomas. 2016. "'Violence Against Children Sells Very Well'. Reporting Crime in the Media and Attitudes to Punishment." Pp. 923–947 in *Women and Children as Victims and Offenders: Background, Prevention, Reintegration*, edited by Helmut Kury, Sławomir Redo, and Evelyn Shae. Zurich: Springer International.

Hetherington, Marc J. 2005. *Why Trust Matters: Declining Political Trust and the Demise of American Liberalism.* Princeton, NJ: Princeton University Press.

Hickel, Jason. 2014. "'Xenophobia' in South Africa: Order, Chaos, and the Moral Economy of Witchcraft." *Cultural Anthropology* 29(1):103–127.

Hiltzik, Michael. 2014. "Rich, Educated and Stupid Parents Are Driving the Vaccination Crisis." *Los Angeles Times*, September 3. Accessed May 21, 2018. www.latimes.com.

Hofstadter, Richard. [1952] 2008. *The Paranoid Style in American Politics.* New York: Vintage Books.

Hollander, Jocelyn A. 2001. "Vulnerability and Dangerousness: The Construction of Gender through Conversation about Violence." *Gender & Society* 15(1):83–109.

Hopkins, Daniel J. and Jonathan M. Ladd. 2014. "The Consequences of Broader Media Choice: Evidence from the Expansion of Fox News." *Quarterly Journal of Political Science* 9(1):115–135.

Hunter, Lance Young, Wesley Lawrence Meares, and Martha Humphries Ginn. 2018. "Terrorism and Voter Turnout in Seven Urban Centers in the United States." *Behavioral Sciences of Terrorism and Aggression* 10(2):110–137.

Hurst, Daniel. 2018. "How the Mother of Japanese Student Shot Dead Became a Force for US Gun Reform." *Guardian*, March 22.

Infowars.com. 2017. "Alex Jones AMA: Aliens, When Will Trump Release the Information?" *Infowars*, November 9. Accessed November 2, 2018. www.infowars.com.

Iyengar, Shanto, Mark D. Peters, and Donald R. Kinder. 1982. "Experimental Demonstrations of the 'Not-so-Minimal' Consequences of Television News Programs." *American Political Science Review* 76(4):848–858.

Iyengar, Shanto, and Sean J. Westwood. 2015. "Fear and Loathing across Party Lines: New Evidence on Group Polarization." *American Journal of Political Science* 59(3):690–707.

Jackson, Jonathan. 2008. "A Psychological Perspective on Vulnerability in the Fear of Crime." *Psychology, Crime and Law* 15(4):2–25.

Jackson, Jonathan, and Emily Gray. 2010. "Functional Fear and Public Insecurities about Crime." *British Journal of Criminology* 50(1):1–22.

Jamieson, Kathleen Hall, and Joseph N. Capella. 2008. *Echo Chamber: Rush Limbaugh and the Conservative Media Establishment*. New York: Oxford University Press.

Janik, Rachel. 2018. "I Laugh at the Death of Normies": How Incels Are Celebrating the Toronto Mass Killing." *Southern Poverty Law Center*, April 24. Accessed October 30, 2018. www.splcenter.org.

Jarymowicz, Maria, and Daniel Bar-Tel. 2006. "The Dominance of Fear over Hope in the Life of Individuals and Collectives." *European Journal of Social Psychology* 36(3):367–392.

Jenaro, Cristina, Noelia Flores, María Gómez-Vela, Francisca González-Gil, and Cristina Caballo. 2007. "Problematic Internet and Cell-Phone Use: Psychological, Behavioral, and Health Correlates." *Addiction Research & Theory* 15(3):309–320.

Jennings, M. Kent, and Laura Stoker. 2004. "Social Trust and Civic Engagement across Time and Generations." *Acta Politica* 39(4):342–379.

Jolley, Daniel, and Karen M. Douglas. 2014. "The Social Consequences of Conspiracism: Exposure to Conspiracy Theories Decreases Intentions to Engage in Politics and to Reduce One's Carbon Footprint." *British Journal of Psychology* 105(1):35–56.

Jong, Jonathan, and Jamin Halberstadt. 2016. *Death Anxiety and Religious Belief: An Existential Psychology of Religion*. London: Bloomsbury.

Jong, Jonathan, Robert Ross, Tristan Philip, Si-Hua Chang, Naomi Simons, and Jamin Halberstadt. 2017. "The Religious Correlates of Death Anxiety: A Systematic Review and Meta-Analysis." *Religion, Brain, and Behavior* 8(1):4–20.

Kanstroom, Daniel. 2007. *Deportation Nation: Outsiders in American History*. Cambridge, MA: Harvard University Press.

Kaplan, Karen. 2015. "Vaccine Refusal Helped Fuel Disneyland Measles Outbreak, Study Says." *Los Angeles Times*, March 16. Accessed April 10, 2019. www.latimes.com.

Kaysing, Bill. 2017. *We Never Went to the Moon: America's Thirty Billion Dollar Swindle*. North Charleston, NC: CreateSpace Independent Publishing Platform.

Kennedy, Merrit. 2016. "Lead-Laced Water in Flint: A Step-by-Step Look at the Makings of a Crisis." *NPR Southern California Public Radio*, April 20.

Kimmel, Michael S., and Matthew Mahler. 2003. "Adolescent Masculinity, Homophobia, and Violence: Random School Shootings, 1982–2001." *American Behavioral Scientist* 46(10):1439–1458.

Kinane, Karolyn, and Michael A. Ryan, eds. 2009. *End of Days: Essays on the Apocalypse from Antiquity to Modernity*. Jefferson, NC. McFarland.

King, Karen E. 2003. *What Is Gnosticism?* Cambridge, MA: Harvard University Press.

Kishi, Katayoun. 2017. "Assaults against Muslims in U.S. Surpass 2001 Level." *Pew Research Center*, November 15. www.pewresearch.org.

Kissell, Rick. 2015. "Cable News Networks Draw Big Friday Audience Following Terrorist Attacks." *Variety*, November 16.

Knight, Peter. 2002. "Introduction: A Nation of Conspiracy Theorists." Pp. 1–20 in *Conspiracy Nation: The Politics of Paranoia in Postwar America*, edited by Peter Knight. New York: NYU Press.

Kohm, Steven A., Courtney A. Waid-Lindberg, Michael Weinrath, Tara O'Connor Shelley and Rhonda R. Dobbs. 2012. "The Impact of Media on Fear of Crime among University Students: A Cross-National Comparison." *Canadian Journal of Criminology and Criminal Justice* 54(1):67–100.

Kort-Butler, Lisa A., and Kelley J. Sittner Hartshorn. 2011. "Watching the Detectives: Crime Programming, Fear of Crime, and Attitudes about the Criminal Justice System." *Sociological Quarterly* 52(1):36–55.

Kostinsky, Spencer, Edward Bixler, and Paul Kettl. 2001. "Threats of School Violence in Pennsylvania after Media Coverage of the Columbine High School Massacre." *Archives of Pediatrics & Adolescent Medicine* 155(9):994–1001.

Krause, Neal. 1991. "Stress and Isolation from Close Ties in Later Life." *Journal of Gerontology* 46(4):183–195.

Kwong, Jessica. 2017. "Alex Jones Calls Las Vegas Massacre 'Phony' and 'Part of this Deal that Trump's Got with the Saudis.'" *Newsweek*, November 28. www.newsweek.com.

Lane, Jodi, Nicole E. Rader, Billy Henson, Bonnie S. Fisher, and David C. May. 2016. *Fear of Crime in the United States: Causes, Consequences, and Contradictions*. Durham, NC: Carolina Academic Press.

Lankford, Adam. 2016a. "Are America's Public Mass Shooters Unique? A Comparative Analysis of Offenders in the United States and Other Countries." *International Journal of Comparative and Applied Criminal Justice* 40(2):171–183.

Lankford, Adam. 2016b. "Fame-seeking Rampage Shooters: Initial Findings and Empirical Predictions." *Aggression and Violent Behavior* 27(March–April):122–129.

Lankford, Adam. 2016c. "Public Mass Shooters and Firearms: A Cross-National Study of 171 Countries." *Violence and Victims* 31(2):187–199.

Lankford, Adam, and Eric Madfis. 2018. "Don't Name Them, Don't Show Them, but Report Everything Else: A Pragmatic Proposal for Denying Mass Killers the Attention They Seek and Deterring Future Offenders." *American Behavioral Scientist* 62(2):260–279.

Lankford, Adam, and Sara Tomek. 2018. "Mass Killings in the United States from 2006 to 2013: Social Contagion or Random Clusters?" *Suicide and Life-Threatening Behavior* 48(4):459–467.

Learner, Jennifer S., and Dachner Keltner. 2001. "Fear, Anger, and Risk." *Journal Personality and Social Psychology* 81(1):146–159.

LeDoux, Joseph E. 2002. "Emotion, Memory and the Brain." *Scientific American* 12(1):62–71.

LeDoux, Joseph E. 2003. "The Emotional Brain, Fear, and the Amygdala." *Cellular and Molecular Neurobiology* 23(4/5):727–738.

LeDoux, Joseph E. 2014. "Coming to Terms with Fear." *Proceedings of the National Academy of Sciences* 114(10):E2016–E2025.

LeDoux, Joseph E. 2017. "Semantics, Surplus Meaning, and the Science of Fear." *Trends in Cognitive Sciences* 21(5):303–306.

LeDoux, Joseph E., and Richard Brown. 2017. "A Higher Order Theory of Emotional Consciousness." *Proceedings of the National Academy of Sciences* 111(8):2871–2878.

LeDoux, Joseph E., and Stefan G. Hoffman. 2018. "The Subjective Experience of Emotion: A Fearful Review." *Current Opinion in Behavioral Sciences* 19:67–72.

LeDoux, Joseph E., and Daniel S. Pine. 2016. "Using Neuroscience to Help Understand Fear and Anxiety: A Two-System Framework." *American Journal of Psychiatry* 173(11):1083–1093.

Lee, Min Sik, and Jeffrey T. Ulmer. 2000. "Fear of Crime among Korean Americans in Chicago Communities." *Criminology* 38(4):1173–1206.

Lee, Vic. 2015. "Bullet that Killed Kate Steinle Appears to Have Ricocheted." *ABC 7 News*, August 26. Accessed Feb. 22, 2018. http://abc7news.com.

Lee, Vic, and Chris Nguyen. 2015. "Family Devastated after Woman Shot, Killed in SF." *ABC7 San Francisco*, July 8. Accessed February 21, 2018. http://abc7news.com.

Lepp, Andrew, Jacob E. Barkley, and Aryn C. Karpinski. 2014. "The Relationship between Cell Phone Use, Academic Performance, Anxiety, and Satisfaction with Life in College Students." *Computers in Human Behavior* 31:343–350.

Lipschultz, Jeremy H., and Michael L. Hilt. 2002. *Crime and Local Television News: Dramatic, Breaking, and Live from the Scene.* Mahwah, NJ: Lawrence Erlbaum Associates.

Liska, Allen E., and Barbara D. Warner. 1991. "Functions of Crime: A Paradoxical Process." *American Journal of Sociology* 96(6):1441–1463.

Live Science Staff. 2012. "Hurricane Sandy Smashes Ocean Wave Records." *Live Science*, November 14. Accessed November 3, 2018. www.livescience.com.

Love, Erik. 2017. *Islamophobia and Racism.* New York: NYU Press.

Mahajan, Neha, and Karen Wynn. 2012. "Origins of 'Us' versus 'Them': Prelinguistic Infants Prefer Similar Others." *Cognition* 124(2):227–233.

Malo, Sebastien. 2018. "Climate Change Threatens Half of U.S. Military Sites: Pentagon." *Reuters*, January 31. Accessed November 3, 2018. www.reuters.com.

Maren, Stephen. 2005. "Building and Burying Fear Memories in the Brain." *Neuroscientist* 11(1):89–99.

Marcus, George E., W. Russell Neuman, and Michael MacKuen. 2000. *Affective Intelligence and Political Judgment*. Chicago: The University of Chicago Press.

Markowitz, Fred E., Paul E. Bellair, Allen E. Liska, and Jianhong Liu. 2001. "Extending Social Disorganization Theory: Modeling the Relationships between Cohesion, Disorder and Fear." *Criminology* 39(2):293–319.

Mason, Fran. 2002. "A Poor Person's Cognitive Mapping." Pp. 40–56 in *Conspiracy Nation: The Politics of Paranoia in Postwar America*, edited by Peter Knight. New York: NYU Press.

Matthews, Todd, Lee Michael Johnson, and Catherine Jenks. 2011. "Does Religious Involvement Generate or Inhibit Fear of Crime?" *Religions* 2(4):485–503.

May, David C. 2001. "The Effect of Fear of Sexual Victimization on Adolescent Fear of Crime." *Sociological Spectrum* 21(2):141–174.

McClatchy-Tribune News Service. 2018. "National Digest: Judge Dismisses Lawsuit Related to Pulse Shooting." *Washington Post*, October 21.

McKee, Kevin J., and Caroline Milner. 2000. "Health, Fear of Crime and Psychosocial Functioning in Older People." *Journal of Health Psychology* 5(4):473–486.

Meindl, James N., and Jonathan W. Ivy. 2017. "Mass Shootings: The Role of the Media in Promoting Generalized Imitation." *American Journal of Public Health* 107(3):368–370.

Melley, Timothy. 2002. "Agency Panic and the Culture of Conspiracy." Pp. 57–84 in *Conspiracy Nation: The Politics of Paranoia in Postwar America*, edited by Peter Knight. New York: NYU Press.

Meyer, Marvin. 2005. *The Gnostic Gospels of Jesus: The Definitive Collection of Mystical Gospels and Secret Books about Jesus of Nazareth*. New York: HarperCollins.

Miller, Matthew, Deborah Azrael, and David Hemenway. 2002. "Rates of Household Firearm Ownership and Homicide Across US Regions and States, 1988–1997." *American Journal of Public Health* 92(12):1988–1993.

Miller, Matthew, David Hemenway, and Deborah Azrael. 2007. "State-level Homicide Victimization Rates in the US in Relation to Survey Measures of Household Firearm Ownership, 2001–2003." *Social Science & Medicine* 64(3):656–664.

Mitchell, Joshua L., and Brendan Toner. 2016. "Exploring the Foundations of US State-Level Anti-Sharia Initiatives." *Politics & Religion* 9(4):720–743.

Moons, Michelle. 2015. "Murderer: I Chose SF because it Is a Sanctuary City." *Breitbart*, July 6. Accessed February 21, 2018. www.breitbart.com.

Moore, Simon, and Jonathan Shepherd. 2007. "The Elements and Prevalence of Fear." *British Journal of Criminology* 47(1):154–162.

Montopoli, Brian. 2010. "Tennessee Lt. Gov. Ron Ramsey Questions Whether Islam Is a Religion." *CBS News*, July 26.

Morain, Dan. 2015. "San Francisco Jailers Dumped a Prisoner and Kathryn Steinle Died." *Sacramento Bee*, July 13. Accessed February 21, 2018. www.sacbee.com.

Morgan, Rachel E., and Grace Kena. 2017. *Criminal Victimization, 2016*. Washington, DC: Bureau of Justice Statistics. Accessed November 8, 2018. www.bjs.gov

Morgan, Michael, and James Shanahan. 2010. "The State of Cultivation." *Journal of Broadcasting & Electronic Media* 54(2):337–355.

Morone, James A. 2003. *Hellfire Nation: The Politics of Sin in American History*. New Haven, CT: Yale University Press.

Morris, Jonathan S. 2007. "Slanted Objectivity? Perceived Media Bias, Cable News Exposure, and Political Attitudes." *Social Science Quarterly* 88(3):707–728.

"Mother of Woman Killed on San Francisco Pier Says Trump Using Death 'for His Political Platform.'" 2015. *Fox News*, July 7. Accessed February 21, 2018. www.foxnews .com.

Nacos, Brigitte L., Yaeli Block-Elkon, and Robert Y. Shapiro. 2011. *Selling Fear: Counterterrorism, the Media and Public Opinion*. Chicago: University of Chicago Press.

Nellis, Ashley Marie and Joanne Savage. 2012. "Does Watching the News Affect Fear of Terrorism? The Importance of Media Exposure on Terrorism Fear." *Crime and Delinquency* 58(5):748–768.

Newport, Frank. 2017a. "Four in 10 Americans Fear Being a Victim of a Mass Shooting." *Gallup*, October 18. Accessed October 31, 2018. http://news.gallup.com.

Newport, Frank. 2017b. "Americans' Fear of Walking Alone Ties 52-Year Low." *Gallup*, November 2. Accessed October 31, 2018. http://news.gallup.com.

Newton, Kenneth. 2001. "Trust, Social Capital, Civil Society, and Democracy." *International Political Science Review* 22(2):201–214.

Nevett, Joshua. 2017. "Moon Landing HOAX? Bombshell Claims 'NASA Admitted 1969 Mission Is NOT Possible.'" *Daily Star*, August 3. Accessed October 21, 2018. www.dailystar.co.uk.

Öhman, Arne. 2005. "The Role of the Amygdala in Human Fear: Automatic Detection of Threat." *Psychoneuroendocrinology* 30(10):953–958.

Öhman, Arne. 2008. "Fear and Anxiety: Overlaps and Distinctions." Pp. 709–729 in *Handbook of Emotions*, edited by Michael Lewis, Jeannette M. Haviland-Jones, and Lisa Feldman Barrett. New York: Guilford Press.

Öhman, Arne. 2009. "Of Snakes and Faces: An Evolutionary Perspective on the Psychology of Fear." *Scandinavian Journal of Psychology* 50(6):543–552.

Öhman, Arne, Katrina Carlsson, Daniel Lundqvist, and Martin Ingvar. 2007. "On the Unconscious Subcortical Origin of Human Fear." *Physiology and Behavior* 92(1–2):180–185.

Öhman, Arne, Anders Flykt, and Francisco Esteves. 2001. "Emotion Drives Attention: Detecting the Snake in the Grass." *Journal of Experimental Psychology* 130(3):466–478.

Öhman, Arne, Daniel Lundqvist, and Francisco Esteves. 2001. "The Face in the Crowd Revisited: A Threat Advantage with Schematic Stimuli." *Journal of Personality and Social Psychology* 80(3):381–396.

Öhman, Arne, and Susan Mineka. 2001. "Fears, Phobias, and Preparedness: Toward an Evolved Module of Fear and Fear Learning." *Psychological Review* 108(3):483–522.

Oliver, J. Eric, and Thomas J. Wood. 2014a. "Conspiracy Theories and the Paranoid Style(s) of Mass Opinion." *American Journal of Political Science* 58(4):952–966.

Oliver, J. Eric, and Thomas J. Wood. 2014b. "Medical Conspiracy Theories and Health Behaviors in the United States." *JAMA Internal Medicine* 174(5):817–818.

Olsson, Andreas, Jeffrey P. Ebert, Mahzarin R. Banaji, and Elizabeth A. Phelps. 2005. "The Role of Social Groups in the Persistence of Learned Fear." *Science* 309(5735):785–787.

Oudekerk, Barbara A., and Jennifer L. Truman. 2017. *Repeat Violent Victimization, 2005–14*. Washington, DC: Bureau of Justice Statistics.

Ousey, Graham C., and Charis E. Kubrin. 2009. "Exploring the Connection between Immigration and Violent Crime Rates in U.S. Cities, 1980–200." *Social Problems* 56(3):447–473.

Ousey, Graham C., and Charis E. Kubrin. 2014. "Immigration and the Changing Nature of Homicide in US Cities." *Journal of Quantitative Criminology* 30(3):453–483.

Pain, Rachel. 2000. "Place, Social Relations and Fear of Crime: A Review." *Progress in Human Geography* 24(3):365–387.

Palamar, Joseph. 2018. "Flakka Is a Dangerous Drug, but it Doesn't Turn You into a Zombie." *The Conversation*, June 12. Accessed October 16, 2018. http://thecon versation.com.

Pappas, Stephanie. 2011. "No Show? Preacher's Doomsday Prediction Echoes Past Failures." *Live Science*, October 22. Accessed November 4, 2018. www.livescience .com.

Pappas, Stephanie. 2017. "Experts Call for Mass Killers' Names to Be Kept Quiet." *Live Science*, October 4. Accessed November 4, 2018. www.livescience.com.

Pearson, Amber L., and Gregory D. Breetzke. 2014. "The Association between the Fear of Crime, and Mental and Physical Wellbeing in New Zealand." *Social Indicators Research* 119(1):281–294.

Peele, Thomas. 2016. "Kate Steinle Killing: Ballistics Expert Calls Fatal Shot Accident." *Mercury News*, August 12. Accessed February 21, 2018. www.mercurynews.com.

Petrosky, Emiko, Janet M. Blair, Carter J. Betz, Katharine A. Fowler, Shane P. D. Jack, and Bridget H. Lyons. 2017. "Racial and Ethnic Differences in Homicides of Adult Women and the Role of Intimate Partner Violence—United States, 2003–2014." *Morbidity and Mortality Weekly Report* 66(28):741–746.

Pew Research Center. 2013. *The State of the News Media 2013*. Washington DC: Pew Research Center.

Piketty, Thomas. 2014. *Capital in the Twenty-First Century*. Cambridge, MA: Harvard University Press.

Pipes, Daniel. 1997. *Conspiracy: How the Paranoid Style Flourishes and Where it Comes From*. New York: The Free Press.

"The Plan." n.d. *Don't Name Them*. Accessed October 29, 2018. www.dontnamethem.org.

Poindexter, Sandra, and Paloma Esquivel. 2014. "Plunge in Kindergartners' Vaccination Rate Worries Health Officials." *Los Angeles Times*, September 2. Accessed May 21, 2018. www.latimes.com.

Powell, Kimberly A. 2011. "Framing Islam: An Analysis of U.S. Media Coverage of Terrorism Since 9/11." *Communication Studies* 62(1):90–112.

Powell, Kimberly A. 2018. "Framing Islam/Creating Fear: An Analysis of U.S. Media Coverage of Terrorism from 2011–2016." *Religions* 9(9):257–273.

Prepper Shows USA. 2018. *Prepper, Survivalist and Self-Reliance Shows.* Accessed November 3, 2018. www.preppershowsusa.com.

Putnam, Robert D. 2001. *Bowling Alone: The Collapse and Revival of American Community.* New York: Simon & Schuster.

"Q & A with Our Founders." 2018. *No Notoriety*, October 2. Accessed October 29, 2018. https://nonotoriety.com.

Rader, Nicole E. 2007. "The Threat of Victimization: A Theoretical Reconceptualization of Fear of Crime." *Sociological Spectrum* 24(6):689–704.

Rader, Nicole E. 2008. "Gendered Fear Management Strategies: Intersections of Doing Gender and Fear Management Strategies in Women's Lives." *Sociological Focus* 41(1):34–52.

Rader, Nicole E., and Stacy H. Raynes. 2014. "Avoidance, Protective, and Weapons Behaviors: An Examination of Constrained Behaviors and their Impact on Concerns about Crime." *Journal of Crime and Justice* 32(2):197–213.

Rader, Nicole E., Jeralynn S. Cossman, and Jeremy R. Porter. 2012. "Fear of Crime and Vulnerability: Using a National Survey of Americans to Examine Two Competing Paradigms." *Journal of Criminal Justice* 40(2):134–141.

Raymond, Adam. 2018. "Alex Jones: Trump Has Called Me 3 Times in the Last Few Months." *New York Magazine*, January 24.

Reed, Andra J., Michael E. Mann, Kerry A. Emanuel, Ning Lin, Benjamin P. Horton, Andrew C. Kemp, and Jeffrey P. Donnelly. 2015. "Increased Threat of Tropical Cyclones and Coastal Flooding to New York City during the Anthropogenic Era." *Proceedings of the National Academy of Sciences* 112(41):12610–2615.

Reid, Lesley Williams, and Miriam Konrad. 2004. "The Gender Gap in Fear: Assessing the Interactive Effects of Gender and Perceived Risk on Fear of Crime." *Sociological Spectrum* 24(4):399–425.

Rengifo, Andres F., and Amanda Bolton. 2012. "Routine Activities and Fear of Crime: Specifying Individual-level Mechanisms." *European Journal of Criminology* 9(2):99–119.

Rice, Doyle. 2018. "2017's Three Monster Hurricanes—Harvey, Irma and Maria— among Five Costliest Ever." *USA Today*, January 30.

Robertson, David G. 2016. *UFOs, Conspiracy Theories and the New Age: Millennial Conspiracism.* London: Bloomsbury.

Robin, Corey. 2004. *Fear: The History of a Political Idea.* Oxford: Oxford University Press.

Robinson Jennifer, Brian A. Lawton, Ralph B. Taylor, and Douglas D. Perkins. 2003. "Multilevel Longitudinal Impacts of Incivilities: Fear of Crime, Expected Safety, and Block Satisfaction." *Journal of Quantitative Criminology* 19(3):237–274.

Roche, Sean Patrick, Justin T. Pickett, and Marc Gertz. 2016. "The Scary World of Online News? Internet News Exposure and Public Attitudes toward Crime and Justice." *Journal of Quantitative Criminology* 32(2):215–326.

Rosenberg, Eli. 2016. "Roberta's, Popular Brooklyn Restaurant, Is Pulled into 'Pizzagate' Hoax." *New York Times*, December 7.

Rosenberg, Eli. 2017. "Alex Jones Apologizes for Promoting 'Pizzagate' Hoax." *New York Times*, March 25.

Rountree, Pamela W., and Kenneth C. Land. 1996. "Perceived Risk versus Fear of Crime: Empirical Evidence of Conceptually Distinct Reactions in Survey Data." *Social Forces* 74(4):1353–1376.

Ruddell, Rick, and Martin G. Urbina. 2004. "Minority Threat and Punishment: A Cross-National Analysis." *Justice Quarterly* 21(4):903–931.

Sampson, Robert J., Stephen W. Raudenbush, and Felton Earls. 1997. "Neighborhoods and Violent Crime: A Multilevel Study of Collective Efficacy." *Science* 277(5328):918–924.

Sanchez, Ray. 2018. "Nearly Half a Million in Puerto Rico Still in the Dark 4 Months after Hurricane Maria." *CNN*, January 25. Accessed November 3, 2018. www.cnn.com.

Sanchez, Ray, Khushbu Shah, and Leyla Santiago. 2018. "FEMA Ending Food and Water Shipments to Puerto Rico, Official Says." *CNN*, January 31. Accessed November 3, 2018. www.cnn.com.

Scarborough, Brittney K., Toya Z. Like-Haislip, Kenneth J. Novak, Wayne L. Lucas, and Leanne F. Alarid. 2010. "Assessing the Relationship between Individual Characteristics, Neighborhood Context and Fear of Crime." *Journal of Criminal Justice* 38(4):819–826.

Showtime. 2017. "San Bernardino, California." *America under Fire*. Aired September 29, 2017. Accessed October 20, 2018. www.sho.com.

Siegel, Michael, Craig S. Ross, and Charles King III. 2013. "The Relationship between Gun Ownership and Firearm Homicide Rates in the United States, 1981–2010." *American Journal of Public Health* 103(11):2098–2105.

Sinclair, Harriet. 2017. "Most Americans Fear Major War under Trump Poll Shows." *Newsweek*, October 19. Accessed October 31, 2018. www.newsweek.com.

Skogan, Wesley. 1986. "Fear of Crime and Neighborhood Change." Pp. 203–209 in *Community and Crimes*, edited by Albert Reiss Jr. and Michael Tonry. Chicago: University of Chicago Press.

Skogan, Wesley G. 1995. "Crime and the Racial Fears of White Americans." *Annals of the American Academy of Political and Social Science* 539(1):59–71.

Skogan, Wesley G., and Michael G. Maxfield. 1981. *Coping with Crime: Individual and Neighborhood Reactions*. Newbury Park, CA: Sage Publications.

Slavo, Mac. 2017. "Liberal Preppers Ready for Trumpocalypse: 'Tired of Being Seen as Wusses Who Won't Survive SHTF'" *SHTFPlan.com*, January 17. Accessed November 3, 2018. www.shtfplan.com.

Smietana, Bob. 2014. "Murfreesboro Mosque Fight Laid to Rest after Supreme Court Ruling." *Washington Post*, June 3.

Smith, Tom W., Jibum Kim, and Jaesok Son. 2017. "Public Attitudes toward Climate Change and Other Environmental Issues across Countries." *International Journal of Sociology* 47(1):62–80.

Solon, Olivia. 2017. "More than 70% of US Fears Robots Taking over Our Lives, Survey Finds." *Guardian*, October 4. Accessed October 31, 2018. www.theguardian.com.

Sorensen, Susan B., Julie G. Peterson Manz, and Richard A. Berk. 1998. "News Media Coverage and the Epidemiology of Homicide." *American Journal of Public Health* 88(10):1510–1514.

Spakovsky, Hans Von, and Rachel S. Landsman. 2015. "San Francisco Aided and Abetted the Murder of Kate Steinle." *Daily Signal*, July 8. Accessed February 21, 2018. http://dailysignal.com.

Stack, Liam. 2016. "He Calls Hillary Clinton a 'Demon.' Who Is Alex Jones?" *New York Times*, October 13.

Stafford, Mai, Tarani Chandola, and Michael Marmot. 2007. "Association between Fear of Crime and Mental Health and Physical Functioning." *American Journal of Public Health* 97(11):2076–2081.

Straub, Frank, Jennifer Zeunik, and Ben Gorban. 2017. "Lessons Learned from the Police Response to the San Bernardino and Orlando Terrorist Attacks." *CTC Sentinel* 10(5):1–7. https://ctc.usma.edu.

Stevens, Matt, Thomas Fuller, and Caitlin Dickerson. 2017. "Trump Tweets 'Build the Wall' after Immigrant Is Acquitted in Kathryn Steinle Case." *New York Times*, November 30. Accessed February 21, 2018. www.nytimes.com.

Sundstrom, Ronald R., and David Haekwon Kim. 2014. "Xenophobia and Racism." *Critical Philosophy of Race* 2(1):20–45.

Sunstein, Cass R. 2005. *Laws of Fear: Beyond the Precautionary Principle*. New York: Cambridge University Press.

Takim, Liyakat. 2011. "The Ground Zero Mosque Controversy: Implications for American Islam." *Religions* 2(2):132–144.

Tallis, Frank, Graham C. L. Davey, and Nicola Capuzzo. 1994. "The Phenomenology of Non-pathological Worry: A Preliminary Investigation." Pp. 61–89 in *Wiley Series in Clinical Psychology: Perspectives on Theory, Assessment and Treatment*, edited by Graham C. L. Day and Frank Tallis. Oxford, England: John Wiley & Sons.

Thatcher, Margaret. 1985. Speech to American Bar Association. Albert Hall, South Kensington, Central London, July 15. Margaret Thatcher Foundation Archive. Accessed April 11, 2019. https://www.margaretthatcher.org/.

Thomas, William I., and Dorothy Swaine Thomas. 1928. *The Child in America: Behavior Problems and Programs*. New York: Knopf.

Tiedens, Larissa Z., and Susan Linton. 2001. "Judgment under Emotional Certainty and Uncertainty: The Effects of Specific Emotions on Information Processing." *Journal of Personality and Social Psychology* 81(6):973–988.

Towers, Sherry, Andres Gomez-Lievano, Maryam Khan, Anuj Mubayi, and Carlos Castillo-Chavez. 2015. "Contagion in Mass Killings and School Shootings." *PLoS One* 10(7):e0117259. https://doi.org/10.1371/journal.pone.0117259.

Tudor, Andrew. 2003. "A (Macro) Sociology of Fear?" *The Sociological Review* 51(2):238–256.

Uddin, Asma T., and Dave Pantzer. 2018. "A First Amendment Analysis of Anti-Sharia Initiatives." *First Amendment Law Review* 10(2):363–418.

U.S. Congress. 2009. House Armed Services Committee Hearing. *Threat Posed by Electromagnetic Pulse (EMP) Attack.* 110th Congress, 2nd Session, July 10, 2018. Washington, DC: U.S. Government Printing Office. Accessed April 11, 2019. https://fas.org.

Unnever, James D., Francis T. Cullen, and Brandon K. Applegate. 2005. "Turning the Other Cheek: Reassessing the Impact of Religion on Punitive Ideology." *Justice Quarterly* 22(3):304–339.

Vales, Leinz. 2016. "Anderson Cooper's Emotional Tribute to Victims." *CNN*, June 14. Accessed October 29, 2018. www.cnn.com.

Victor, Jeffrey S. 1993. *Satanic Panic: The Creation of Contemporary Legend.* Chicago: Open Court.

Vosoughi, Soroush, Deb Roy, and Sinan Ara. 2018. "The Spread of True and False News Online." *Science* 359(6380):1146–1151.

Wallace, Lacey N. 2015. "Responding to Violence with Guns: Mass Shootings and Gun Acquisition." *Social Science Journal* 52(2):156–167.

Wang, Xia. 2012. "Undocumented Immigrants as Perceived Criminal Threat: A Test of the Minority Threat Perspective." *Criminology* 50(3):743–76.

Ward, Charlotte, and David Voas. 2011. "The Emergence of Conspirituality." *Journal for the Contemporary Study of Religion* 26(1):103–121.

Warr, Mark, 1984. "Fear of Victimization: Why Are Women and the Elderly More Afraid?" *Social Science Quarterly* 65(3):681–702.

Weitzer, Ronald, and Charis E. Kubrin. 2004. "Breaking News: How Local TV News and Real-world Conditions Affect Fear of Crime." *Justice Quarterly* 21(3):497–520.

Welch, Michael. 2006. *Scapegoats of September 11th: Hate Crimes & State Crimes in the War on Terror.* Rutgers, NJ: Rutgers University Press.

Wemple, Erik. 2015. "CNN's Anderson Cooper, Too, Has Baffling Shooter-naming Policies." *Washington Post*, December 8.

Wendling, Mike. 2018. "Toronto Van Attack: What Is an 'Incel'?" *BBC News*, April 24. Accessed October 31, 2018. www.bbc.com.

Whitehead, Andrew L., Samuel L. Perry, and Joseph O. Baker. 2018. "Make American Christian Again: Christian Nationalism and Voting for Donald Trump in the 2016 Presidential Election." *Sociology of Religion* 79(2):147–171.

Williams, Michael A. 1996. *Rethinking 'Gnosticism': An Argument for Dismantling a Dubious Category.* Princeton, NJ: Princeton University Press.

Williamson, Elizabeth. 2018. "Judge Rules Against Alex Jones and Infowars in Sandy Hook Lawsuit." *New York Times*, August 30.

Wimmer, Andreas. 1997. "Explaining Xenophobia and Racism: A Critical Review of Current Research Approaches." *Ethnic and Racial Studies* 20(1):17–41.

Wojcik, Daniel. 1997. *The End of the World as We Know It: Faith, Fatalism, and Apocalypse in America.* New York: New York University Press.

Woldoff, Rachael. 2006. "Emphasizing Fear of Crime in Models of Neighborhood Social Disorganization." *Crime Prevention and Community Safety* 8(4):228–247.

Wolniewicz, Claire A., Mojisola F. Tiamiyu, Justin W. Weeks, and Jon D. Elhai. 2018. "Problematic Smartphone Use and Relations with Negative Affect, Fear of Missing Out, and Fear of Negative and Positive Evaluation." *Psychiatry Research* 262:618–623.

Woods, Heather C., and Holly Scott. 2016. "#Sleepyteens: Social Media Use in Adolescence is Associated with Poor Sleep Quality, Anxiety, Depression and Low Self-esteem." *Journal of Adolescence* 51:41–49.

Woodward, Bob. 2018. *Fear: Trump in the White House*. New York: Simon & Schuster.

Wynne, Tom. 2008. "An Investigation into the Fear of Crime: Is there a Link between the Fear of Crime and the Likelihood of Victimization?" *Internet Journal of Criminology*, 1–29. https://docs.wixstatic.com/ugd/b93dd4_75c4b57d5e6f404eboc60596e3113195.pdf

Yazdiha, Haj. 2014. "Law as Movement Strategy: How the Islamophobia Movement Institutionalizes Fear through Legislation." *Social Movement Studies* 13(2):267–274.

Zarefsky, David. 1984. "Conspiracy Arguments in the Lincoln–Douglas Debates." *Journal of the American Forensic Association* 21(2):63–75.

Zarembo, Alan. 2016. "Are the Media Complicit in Mass Shootings?" *Los Angeles Times*, June 18. Accessed October 21, 2018. www.latimes.com.

Zimmerman, Shannon, Luisa Ryan, and David Duriesmith. 2018. *Recognizing the Violent Extremist Ideology of 'Incels'* (Policy Brief). Washington, DC: Women in International Security.

# INDEX

Aamodt, Mike, 93

ABC News, 100, 149n29

Adamski, George, 47

African Americans: conservative fears of, 18, 140n13; conspiracy beliefs of, 42; criminal punitiveness of, 107; criminal victimization fears of, 97, 107; homicide rates in death of, 97; religiosity relation to prejudice against, 26; Sum of All Fears level for, 29; violence experienced by, 91, 97, 107

age, 17; conspiracy beliefs relation to, 42; criminal victimization fear relation to, 28; Sum of all Fears relation to, 24–25, 28; vulnerabilities with, 149n22. *See also* elderly

air pollution fears, 68, *68*

alien presence/encounters: conspiracy theories about, 37–38, *38*, 41, 44, 47–48, 50, 143n43; moon landing and, 37

animal rights extremists, fear of, 18, *20*

animals, fear of, *17*

anti-abortion groups, 18–19, *20*

Antichrist beliefs, 33, 69, 146n25

anti-immigration groups, fear of, 18, *20*, 22, 23

anti-tax groups, 18, *20*, 23

anti-vaccination movement, 13–16

anxiety: with conspiratorial thinking, 113–14, 129; in health consequences of fear, 4, 19, 77, 113–14, 123–24, 129, 131, 133, 134; media consumption role in, 57, 133, 134

Apocalypse/end of the world fears, 69–72, *70, 71. See also* preppers; Shit Hits the Fan preppers

Apollo moon landing. *See* moon landing conspiracies

Arnold, Kenneth, 45–46, 143n45

atheists: fears for, 25, *70*, 71, 141n27; health and well-being relationship with, 26, 27; public opinion of, 84

Austen, Rick and Jane, 59–61

autism, 13, 14–15

Barker, Gray, 46

bath salts-related crimes, 99–100

Bender, Albert K., 45–46

Biblical literalists, 18, 39, 43, 70, 104

Blavatsky, Helena, 47

Boden, Stewart, 74

Branch Davidian standoff (1993), 50–52

Bush, George H. W., 48

Bush, George W., 49

Butter, Michael, 35

Camping, Harold, 69

Carter, Jimmy, 48

Catholics, 19, 25, 70, *70*, 104

cell phones. *See* smartphone use

Centers for Disease Control and Prevention, 13, 97–98

Chapman University Survey of American Fears (CSAF): about, 6–7, 14, 140nn37–38, 148n13; on Apocalypse causes and fear level, 71, *71*; conspiracy theories parameters and findings of, 37–42, *38*, 44, 54, 143nn29–30, 143n37, 145n71, 151nn5–7; on disaster fears and preparedness, 62–63, *63, 64*, 69; 2016 top ten fears, 7, 10–11, *11*, 108; 2017, 6, 140n10; 2018, 7, *8–10*, 10–11, 54, 67–68, 120, 145n71; on vaccinations, 14–15

health and well-being, 7; consequences of
fear impact on, 4, 19, 77, 109–10, 113–14,
123–25, *124*, 129, 131, 133–35, 152n28;
conspiracism impact on, 113–14,
128–29; religiosity curvilinear relationship with, 26, 27. *See also* anxiety
help, giving and receiving. *See* Good
Samaritan actions
Hispanics, fears for, 19, 29, 42, 97, *105*
homicide: fear role in unintentional,
91–92; murder definition compared
with, 149n26; rates and statistics, 3,
97–98. *See also* criminal victimization
fear; shootings and mass murders
Houser, Hal, 73
hurricanes, 64–66

ICE. *See* Immigration and Customs
Enforcement
Illuminati. *See* New World Order/
Illuminati
immigrants: crime rate for native-born
compared with, 3; Jones rhetoric
against, 55; Trump xenophobic treatment of, 119–20; undocumented, 1–4,
18, *20*, 23; xenophobia of, 88–89, 117,
119–22, 132, 147n58. *See also* anti-
immigration groups, fear of
Immigration and Customs Enforcement
(ICE), 1, 3
incarceration policies, 107, 129–30
Incel Rebellion, 78–79
income, 17; anti-vaccination beliefs relation
to, 14, 15; media coverage of homicide
relation to victims, 98; social vulnerability and fear relation to, 28–29; Sum
of all Fears relation to, 24–25
InfoWars, 51, 53–56, *55*, 144n60
Islamic extremists, 18, *20*, 76
Islamophobia: declines from 2016 to 2018,
88; media/news consumption role in,
83–89; mosques and Islamic community centers opposition with, 84–85,

87, 88; political orientation relation
to, 86–88; state statutes reflecting,
84; terrorism fear relation to, 86–88;
Trump role in, 84, 85, 86, 87, 88, 119,
121; xenophobia relation to, 83, 88–89,
119, 147n58
isolation, 4, 109–10, 125, 135

Jackson, Seth, 52
Jenkins, Jerry, 69
Jews: fears for, 25, 70, *70*, 104; xenophobic
attacks on, 118
JFK assassination: conspiratorial beliefs
about, 33, 38, *38*, 40, 41, 48, 50, 54;
Jones on, 50; Wilcock on, 48
Johnston, Ken, 31–32, 36–37
Jones, Alex: conspiracy theories and
ideology of, 50–56, *55*, 128; InfoWars,
51, 53–56, *55*, 144n60; profile and
predictors for supporters of, 54–56, *55*,
143n40; Trump support and relationship with, 53–54, 128
Joplin, Missouri, 63–64

Kaysing, Bill, 142
Kennedy, John F. *See* JFK assassination

Lankford, Adam, 79–80
Las Vegas shooting (2017), 51, 94
LeDoux, Joseph, 5
Left Behind series, 69
left-wing extremists, fear of, 18, *20*
liberal fears: conservatives fears divide
from, 19, *20*; Islamophobia and, 87–88;
MSNBC watching relation to, 23, *23*;
personal profile and predictors for,
18–19; top common, *17*, 18, *20*, 23
Lincoln, Abraham, 48
*Louder Than Words* (McCarthy), 13

Madden, Mike, 73
Madfis, Eric, 79–80
Martin, Trayvon, 91

paranormalism: in conspiracy theories, role of, 41, 44–45, *45*, 54, 143nn30–31, 143n43; Jones ideology and, 50, 55; religiosity curvilinear relationship with, 26–27

Paris Climate Accords, 7, 69

Peairs, Rodney, 91

personal tragedies, *17*

phobias, *17*

Pittsburgh Jewish temple shooting (2018), 118

Pizzagate, 51

political orientation, 140n12; fears comparison and divide based on, 19, *20*; fears most commonly related to, *17*, 17–19, *20*, 23; Islamophobia relation to, 86–88; Jones InfoWars believers relation to, 55; media/news consumption and fear relation to, 21–24, *22*, *23*; neurology behind fears based on, 19, 21; preppers, 66–67; religion relation to fears based on, 18–19; Sum of all Fears relation to, 24–25; xenophobia relation to, 120–21, *121*, 153n12. *See also* conservative fears; liberal fears

pollution fears, 7, 16, *17*, 67–69, *68*

Poppo, Ronald, 99–100

power/powerlessness: consequences of fear education impact on, 12, 133–35; conspiracy theories and role of, 33–34, 36, 41

prejudice, religiosity relationship with, 26, 141n32

Prepper Camp (2014), 61–62

preppers (survivalists): Apocalypse fear for, 71–72; on EMP grid shutdown, 59–60, 61; political orientation of, 66–67; self-reliance ideology of, 65, 72, 128; skills and ingenuity of, 60–62; terminology preference for, 145n1. *See also* Shit Hits the Fan preppers

property crime fear, 94, *94*; previous victimization role in, 96, 105–6, 117; religiosity relation to, 103

Protestants: Apocalypse fears of, 70, *70*; conspiracy theory beliefs of, 43; criminal victimization fear of, 104; political fears of, 19; Sum of All Fears level for, 25, 141n27

public spaces fear, 4, 78, 111, 125

punitiveness. *See* criminal punitiveness

race/ethnicity, 17; in conservative fears profile, 18, 140n13; conspiracy believers predictive profile on, 42; criminal punitiveness relation to, 107, 150n57; criminal victimization fear relation to, 97, 107; Good Samaritan actions relation to, 152n13; Jones InfoWars support relation to, 55; liberal fears profile and, 18–19; media coverage of homicide relation to victims, 98; religiosity relation to prejudice of, 26, 141n32; social vulnerability and fear relation to, 97; Sum of all Fears relation to, 24–25, 29–30

Ramirez, Jose, 99

Reagan, Ronald, 48

Regalado, Tomás, 65–66

region of country, fears relation to, 17, 24–25, 63, *64*

religion and religiosity, 17, 140n8, 140n11; Apocalypse fears relation to, *70*, 70–71; biblical literalists fear and, 18, 39, 43, 70, 104; conspiracy theories relation with, 33–34, 39, 41, 43; criminal victimization fear relation to, 102–4, 149n32, 150n48; curvilinear effect of fear with, 25–27, 141n32; death fear relation to, 26; Good Samaritan actions relation to, 152n13–14; health and well-being relationship with, 26, 27; paranormalism relationship with, 26–27; political orientation-based fears and, 18–19; prejudice relationship with, 26, 141n32; Sum of All Fears impacted by, 25–27, 141n27

Woodward, Bob, 119
World War II conspiracies, 48, 144n53

xenophobia: consequences of, 4, 117–23; conspiracy theory supporters relation to, 55–56, 143n30, 143n40; criminal punitiveness beliefs relation to, 107, 119–20, 122–23, 129–30; for Fox News audience, 153n12; of immigrants, 88–89, 117, 119–22, 132, 147n58; Islamophobia relation to, 83, 88–89, 119, 147n58; Jones

InfoWars ideology and, 55, 56; neurology of, 117–18, 132; political orientation relation to, 120–21, *121*, 153n12; racism contrasted with, 117; of Trump policies and supporters, 119–22, *122*, 130, 152n23. *See also* Islamophobia

YouTube, 52–54, 79

Zeigler, Jeffrey, 91
Zimmerman, George, 91

## ABOUT THE AUTHORS

Christopher D. Bader is Professor of Sociology at Chapman University and is affiliated with the Institute for Religion, Economics and Culture. He is an associate director of the Association of Religion Data Archives (www.theArda.com), the world's largest archive of religion survey data, funded by the Templeton Foundation and Lilly Foundation.

Joseph O. Baker is Associate Professor in the Department of Sociology and Anthropology at East Tennessee State University and a senior research associate for the Association of Religion Data Archives. He is the author of *American Secularism*.

L. Edward Day is Associate Professor and Chair of the sociology department at Chapman University. He is co–principal investigator of the ongoing Chapman University Survey of American Fears.

Ann Gordon is Associate Professor of Political Science and Director of the Ludie and David C. Henley Social Science Research Laboratory, Chapman University. She is co–principal investigator of the ongoing Chapman University Survey of American Fears.